1993

The Moral Art
of Dickens

The Moral Art of Dickens

Essays by
Barbara Hardy

ATHLONE

Published by The Athlone Press 1970
44 Bedford Row, London WC1R 4LY
and 51 Washington Street, Dover, NH 03820
Reprinted 1985
© *Copyright 1970 Barbara Hardy*

British Library Cataloguing in Publication Data

Hardy, Barbara
  The moral art of Dickens: essays.
  1. Dickens, Charles, *1812–1870* –Criticism
  and interpretation
  I. Title
  823'.8   PR4588

  ISBN 0–485–11274–4
  ISBN 0–485–12049–6 (pbk.)

Library of Congress Cataloging in Publication Data

Hardy, Barbara Nathan.
  The moral art of Dickens.
  1. Dickens, Charles, 1812–1870—Religion and
ethics.   2. Ethics in literature.   3. Moral conditions in
literature.   I. Title.
PR4592.E8H37   1985   823'.8   85–18554

ISBN 0–485–11274–4
ISBN 0–485–12049–6 (pbk.)

Printed in Great Britain by
Paradigm Print,
Bungay, Suffolk
              196645

To Kate Hardy

Acknowledgements

Part of Chapter 1 is drawn from my British Council Pamphlet, *Charles Dickens: The Later Novels*, Longmans, Green & Co Ltd, 1968. Chapter 2 was first published in *Victorian Studies* in 1961; Chapter 4 in *The London Review* in 1967; Chapter 5 in *Dickens and the Twentieth Century*, ed. J. Gross and G. Pearson, Routledge & Kegan Paul Ltd, 1962; and Chapter 7 in *Essays in Criticism* in 1963. I am grateful to the editors and publishers for their permission to reprint.

I want to express gratitude to Michael Slater, who has read the book and given valuable criticism and advice, and to various students of Birkbeck and Royal Holloway Colleges, with whom I have profitably discussed Dickens. I should also like to record my grateful memories of a happy winter (1964–5) spent in the English Department of the University of Dijon, where I wrote some of this book.

B.H.

Acknowledgements

Contents

Introduction

This book is concerned with Dickens as a moral novelist. I suppose the impulse behind all Victorian and most later novels is moral. The novel usually explores the possible worlds created in memory, anticipation, fantasy, blueprint, revision, and vision in order to probe and discuss meanings and values. In Dickens the moral concern is especially conspicuous, at times a discursive intrusion into the virtual experience created by the art. Behind this conspicuousness lies a constant radical questioning of society, a checking and investigation and discussion of social meaning by fiction, and a violent and moving refusal to enclose art, to shut it off from contemporary life. Increasing the conspicuousness is Dickens's peculiar crudity, a crudity that is both essential to him and valuable in literary experiment. If I have at times seemed to over-stress this crudity by comparing it with the *finesse* and *nuance* of such psychological novelists as George Eliot and Henry James, I should here make it clear that such comparison was not made in the interests of preferential judgment, but in the hope of highlighting Dickens's individuality. It is because I believe that the trend of modern criticism has been to blur the individuality of the artist and the work of art, by stressing those formal and thematic qualities which most works of art hold in common, and by assuming or inferring forms of symbolism both like and unlike Dickensian forms, that I have at times felt it necessary to argue with such critics as J. Hillis Miller and Dorothy Van Ghent. Dickens probably suffers more than George Eliot and Conrad, say, from the critical fictions of total relevance[1] and covert symbolic form,[2] for he is especially close to the explicit and under-distanced modes of acting, oratory, and journalistic address. It seems important, therefore, to stress both his failures and successes. *Martin Chuzzlewit*'s discontinuity of moral action, for instance, and the marvellous particularity of symbol in *Great Expectations*, one a failure, one a success, are both unique and neglected features of the novels and the novelist.

I have also made some initial generalizations about Dickens's attitudes, values and forms in the first Section of the book, which considers the changing shape of his moral art, its varying but always heterogeneous complex form, its different combinations of pessimism and optimism, its combination of fictions about society, past, present, future, and the individual. I have also said something about Dickens's versions of the *Bildungs-roman*: the idea of moral progress and growth is central in his novels, but has to be looked at closely, in the full context of action and psychology, for it is again part of his uniqueness to combine insights with crudity, profundity of theory with perfunctory, superficial or stereotyped realization.

The second Section discusses form, character, and

---

[1] See my discussion in *The Appropriate Form* (London, 1964).
[2] See Chapter 6 below and also Robert Garis, *The Dickens Theatre* (Oxford, 1965).

symbolism in four representative novels: one early, *Pickwick Papers*, two from the middle period, *Martin Chuzzlewit* and *David Copperfield*, and one late, *Great Expectations*. Each of these chapters is concerned with the problems of the individual novel, but always in relation to the larger theme of moral fiction.

The essays in this book have been written over a period of nine years and I have made no attempt to bring references to other critical studies up to date, but have left them as they stood at the completion of each essay, so that my discussion of *Martin Chuzzlewit*, for instance, makes no reference to criticism after 1961, apart from one small footnote gloss in response to P. N. Furbank's comment in the Introduction to his *Penguin* edition of the novel.

Section One

General

I Society and the Individual

I begin with some general observations about Dickens's moral art, before spiralling into a look at his basic pattern of change and conversion, and, eventually, at some of his individual novels. The spiral begins outside and beyond Dickens, for the Victorian art of fiction is essentially a moral art. It questions the nature and purpose of moral action, and at its best, shows the difficulty and complexity of giving, loving, and growing out from self in an unjust, commercialized, and de-naturing society. What distinguishes Dickens's moral questioning from that of Thackeray, Charlotte Brontë, George Eliot, and Hardy, is his combination of social despair and personal faith, his capacity to distrust both society and social reform while retaining and perhaps deepening a faith in the power of human love. Charlotte Brontë and George Eliot are of course concerned to examine moral psychology, and to do so within a defined environment where the facts of class, culture, money, and social grouping are fairly clearly faced. But there is nothing in their novels which involves a determined and radical criticism of society, and even where their characters are seen as so plainly determined by environment as to be socially illustrative, the individual is always in the foreground, society in the background. The initial and continuing impulse is the concern with the individual. Theirs cannot be called a sociological imagination.

Dickens is primarily concerned with the nature of society, and his individual characters are pretty plainly illustrations, created by needs and roles, seen as agents and victims, within a critical analysis of contemporary England. The inappropriateness of the word 'background' when applied to the social detail in Dickens will make the point more rapidly than long discussion. Yet Dickens is quite different from the two great Victorian novelists who are also engaged with the defective society. Thackeray grasps and criticizes society in the medium of satire, Hardy in the medium of tragedy. Both are consistent in their social pessimism, the one beginning and the other closing the damning analysis of Victorian society. Their characters are seen as the social product, as determined wholly by the environment. Even if we start with the ideal or the idealist, Dobbin or Colonel Newcome, Tess or Jude, we end with the ideal tempered, neutralized, qualified, or destroyed. The good deed does not light the naughty world in *Vanity Fair*, *Henry Esmond*, or *Jude the Obscure*, but generally flickers and is quenched. The surviving are the fittest, not the virtuous.

Dickens is interested in the conditioned character, but includes in his fiction a continuing fantasy about the ideal, the unconditional virtue. And in Dickens virtue is often the survivor. His novels show a division between the society he rejects and the humanity he believes in, and that humanity, in different ways, is somehow preserved, frozen, shut off, and saved from the social pressure. One of the main features of his fiction

4

is the double emphasis, on the power and glory of human love, and the power and horror of contemporary society. In the early novels his encapsulated glories are those of angelic children. Oliver, Nell, Barnaby, Paul, and Florence are remarkable in their purity and their effectiveness: they seem to be shut off from corruption but have enough connection with the environment to be able to heal and rescue. The isolated purity is stressed by the darkness and twistedness of the surrounding society.

We see Oliver and Nell, in particular, isolated, wandering, often at night, in the unknown country or city, surrounded by the old, the knowing, the monstrous. Even the virtuous companions like Toots in *Dombey and Son* or Kit in *The Old Curiosity Shop* are grotesque, comic, mis-shapen this way or that. The visual point, made in both text and illustration, is simply expressive of Dickens's intentions. He tells us clearly that he wanted Oliver to represent the strength of virtue in the corrupt world, and tried to show Nell's innocent beauty in a grotesquely curious world. Both novels leave a similar impression of darkness, crowdedness, and oppressiveness, even though much of the action is in the open air. We tend to remember Oliver shut and hemmed in, by ugliness, darkness, nightmare. We remember Nell surrounded by the grotesque players and properties of the Curiosity Shop, the Punch and Judy show, Mrs Jarley's Waxworks, and the strange antiquities of the village where she dies. Much of the grotesque life is moral enough; Mrs Jarley and her excellently adaptable waxworks, for instance, are obviously on the side of the angels, and may have been an effective rehearsal for the circus in *Hard Times*. But the grotesque benevolence joins with the malignancy of Quilp and the industrial inferno to create an environment where the child-character is both thrown into relief and really given life by the surrounding bizarre scene. Purity is isolated, trapped, tested, and defined in a world where evil is properly ugly and twisted but where even virtue tends to be odd, stunted, crazed, even deformed.

This strong contrast is far more than a device for making the threatening and trapping action: the angelic children escape, we ultimately feel their invulnerability. They emerge as made of a different stuff from the rest of the world, and this is indeed the case. Their speech is pure and classless, and their virtue beyond contamination. One of the many interesting things about this intactness of Dickensian virtue is that it is presented in novels which are not only aware of determination, but explicitly concerned with it: the treatment of the different members of the thieves' gang, the comments of Nancy, who truly says she cannot get out of the streets, and the plot to corrupt Oliver, all show Dickens getting the idea of the warped human being right into the centre of his action. He gives us one very cunning scene (in Chapter xviii) where Oliver is almost shown as temptable: he is first cunningly cold-shouldered and then cunningly brought into the family circle, and while he polishes shoes and smiles at jokes, with the susceptibility of the recent return from exile, Dickens gets as close as he ever does to showing us how corruption might work. But there is never a tremor in Oliver.

6

Nell's situation is rather different, for she is threat-
ened by her grandfather's corruptibility, not her own.
Like Oliver she is a strong instance of moral energy,
never weak, never frightened, rising like an angel to
carry off the old man from the temptations of gambling
and theft, and indeed rescuing him back to the world
of love and nature. Oliver is self-redeeming, Nell the
agent of someone else's redemption, but in each case
the virtuous character rises triumphant over all the
threats. Nell's death strengthens the triumph rather
than weakens it.

These two virtuous children are given a reinforce-
ment of Christian pastoral. Dickens sometimes seems
to fall back on pastoral as a surrogate for religion,
though he cannot actually be said to be very sensitive to
either Nature or God. His language is at its weakest,
flattest, and cheapest when dealing with aesthetic and
religious feeling. But the purity, beauty, and as-yet-
intact naturalness of the country is the perfectly
resonant background for the child caught in the city or
running away from it. T. A. Jackson may have a point
in his powerfully tendentious argument about the
irreligiousness of Dickens (*Charles Dickens: the progress
of a radical*, London, 1937), but we cannot conclude too
quickly that where Dickens writes vulgarly he lacks
feeling. Some of the weakest and silliest parts of *Oliver
Twist* and *The Old Curiosity Shop* concern the gardening
activities of the children, their love of flowers, their way
with the birds, their affinity with the crude techni-
colours of Dickens's green world, where Dickens is
quite consistently putting emphasis on the romantically
organic society. Northrop Frye, in his essay, 'Dickens

7

and the Comedy of Humors', in *Experience in the Novel*, *Selected Papers from the English Institute* edited by R. H. Pearce (New York and London, 1968), draws our attention to the kind of characters who tend to gush about Nature in Dickens—Mrs Merdle, Mrs Chick, Wackford Squeers, and, we should add, Edith Dombey's horrible old mother, 'Cleopatra'. Dickens may be revealing in such correlations his lack of feeling for nature, but he certainly used it as typically and broadly significant of the unconditional goodness, as the good image to put against the dark city. Interestingly, the pastoral scenes in these early novels are part of the feeling against institutions. The Dickens countryside is free of the heartless and killing forms of institutional life typical of the towns; such institutions as exist, the church, the village school, are small, romantically organic, unbureaucratic, informed by love not law. The fact that Dickens usually shows religious and educational institutions harshly and critically supports the point.

In neither *Oliver Twist* nor *The Old Curiosity Shop* is the social criticism centrally or clearly directed against the social system, whereas in the novels from *Dombey and Son* onwards there is a firm grasp of a total problem, a grasp which perhaps began to take shape in the fable of *A Christmas Carol*, a very crucial and formative fantasy in Dickens's career. T. A. Jackson puts forward the plausible suggestion that Dickens's early social optimism derived from the flourishing early stage of Chartism, while the pessimism of his late novels may well have been shaped by reactionary triumphs after 1850. But the early optimism was made viable by the purely local nature of the social criticism: the attacks on the new Poor Law in *Oliver Twist*, on industrial hardship and poverty in *The Old Curiosity Shop*, and on appalling schools and child neglect in *Nicholas Nickleby* were powerful but localized. In calling Dickens a novelist of the sociological imagination, which is admittedly an anachronistic term,[1] I have in mind Dickens's use of his novels as a means of coming to know society, and it seems clear that his optimism slowly vanished as his special cases accumulated in number and then created a new kind of social vision and a less answerable problem. It is true that Dickens nowhere confines his attention to one single institution, for even in *Pickwick Papers* he moves from an attack on human follies to a recognition of the folly and injustice of the law, government, and the prison system. But only gradually does he seem to piece together the view of special social abuses into a coherent attack. And by this time there is only despair or an enclosed faith in the human heart.

In *A Christmas Carol*, *Martin Chuzzlewit*, and then most plainly in *Dombey and Son* and thereafter, Dickens comes to see and analyse, as Jackson points out, Marx's cash-nexus and Engels's 'fractionalized man'. His fiction becomes more concerned with the perils of love and virtue, with the deformations of the individual. In the early novels the saints and angels were powerful, but increasingly he comes to show the difficulty of virtue, and some of his most interesting cases of conversion involve a prior study of deteriora-

[1] As W. W. Robson pointed out in a review of *Charles Dickens: The Later Novels* in *The Dickensian*, lxv (1969), 114-16.

tion. The conversions of Dombey and Pip, for instance, are symbolic and optimistic conclusions affirming the possibilities of love as strongly as Oliver and Nell, but the darkness and light, the crooked and straight, are now put within single characters. It is significant that Dombey is analysed as a diseased and nearly destroyed human being. His corruption is imaged in the figure of infection, which can conveniently combine the physical facts of filth and suffering with the symbolism of the moral forces of power, class-division, and cash-values. The uncorrupted children are secluded in ways that Oliver and Nell were not, but only because Dickens uses them to discuss emotional deprivation: they are innocent critics and poor little rich children. But they are also less potent images of the power of love, for Dickens is turning his attention, realistically, to human weakness, to conditions and conditioning.

The chicken-and-egg speculation seems especially pointless in the case of Dickens. His art grew in power and order and single-mindedness as his social vision grew more coherent and profound and more politically aggressive. His genius properly confounds the distinction between aesthetic order and moral order, and we come to feel that all the separate items of criticism and attack in his imaged society are linked by his recognition of the lack of love, justice, nature, and human wholeness, by his shrewd perception of the transformation of moral values into economic ones, and the debasement of human relations and groups. The result is more unified fictions, and a sense of capitalist human sacrifice seen precisely in at least some Marxist ways.

The result is not fully unified novels. There remain

divisions in Dickens. A sense of moral order and economic cause does not guarantee harmony or integrity in art, and it could be argued that where the appreciation of the social whole is clearest and most complex, as in *Bleak House*, the art is more strongly divided. Dickens, like all novelists, and like most human beings in their compulsive and necessary story-telling, can combine a diagnostic narrative analysis with a dream. The harder the look at the worst and the less the faith in political reform, the more powerful the urge towards a human relationship and a human power that can state or even symbolize some hope and faith. It was much easier to imply that workhouses and baby-farms could be improved if their officials had the loving hearts of Maylies and Brownlows than to suggest that Chancery or Tom-All-Alone's could be transformed or abolished by love. In *Bleak House* Dickens seems to see the monstrous inaccessibility of social growth. He comes to see this as he gets to know more, and that knowledge enters the novels in considerable documentary detail— about crime, education, housing, sanitation, law, and so forth. But he comes to see not only the complexity of institutions but the complexity of love.

In *Oliver Twist* and *The Curiosity Shop* all we lacked was love, but where it existed, love was simple in its nature and in its efficiency. In *Bleak House* we see the distortions and displacements of love, the wry facts of the Jellyby and Pardiggle and Carstone motives and feelings. Love can be misplaced and can distort or destroy itself in wanting human order and human happiness. Love can co-exist with ambition and greed, and encourage them. Like Dombey, Mrs Jellyby and

Richard Carstone are fairly complex human beings, by no means monsters, or, if monstrous, sufficiently complex to show their human possibilities. Neither virtue nor vice is made out of different stuff: Richard, unlike Pecksniff, is capable of love and Mrs Jellyby is in some ways, unlike Pecksniff, quite a nice woman.

One could argue that it is the moral successes who remain the weak spots in the novels, despite the growing complexity both of social and psychological insight and embodiment. In *Martin Chuzzlewit* the virtuous characters are Tom Pinch and Mark Tapley, and the novel is concerned to show that adult virtue must expose itself to a look to the worst. Tom is a mixture of child and clown, a descendant of Pickwick, and his loss of innocence is not new, though perhaps more conspicuous than Pickwick's. But it is quickly healed and rewarded. Mark Tapley's attempt to find situations where it will be hard and so creditable to be virtuous is interesting, though it does not add anything except perhaps an emphasis to the idea of virtue's fragility, since he passes all the tests so smoothly. It is one of those many cases in Dickens where we may well feel that the insight is inhibited or blunted by comedy and simplification but that we should be grateful that it at least exists. Something similar happens in cases of characters who are partially role-determined, like Jaggers and Wemmick: they make us feel that Dickens is stereotyping the idea so quickly and tightly that its complexity remains undeveloped, but that a divided Wemmick and Jaggers are at least an advance in the whole notion of the determined or undetermined virtue.

And at least the wall is put up within a single character, and that seems an advance on the walls between comedy and seriousness in *Pickwick Papers*, for instance, where there is the co-existence of jokes about poverty, disease, and death with the anguish of poverty, disease, and death. In *Bleak House* innocence is irrevocably contaminated, and the only feasts in a world where there is so much starvation have to be the heartless feasts of a Chadband. The jokes are very grim, like some of the jokes in Jacobean comedy: the chat about tainted chops before the discovery of Krook's horrible death is designed to increase the revulsion and shock. In the later books there is blending, a transformation of comedy by pathos, horror, and irony, and very few isolated jokes, or wild comic displays like the descriptions of Mr Gamp and Mrs Harris.

It is perfectly clear why *Bleak House* ends as it does, stressing the individual happy-ever-after and its small local efficacy in good housekeeping and good works. We are left with the goodness and cosiness of Esther and Woodhouse, and even the scars of smallpox are transformed: but the book's total exposure leaves the reminder of scars uneffaced, the bleakness of the slums, the terribly bad housekeeping of England. The conclusion is only partially responsive to the rest of the novel, squeezes its solace through too narrow an exit. The reconciliation is a part that will not stand for the whole, either intellectually or emotionally. What we want is an admission of this pocket of love and virtue, (certainly not a transformation of Dickens into Hardy) but together with some expression of irony, sadness, fatigue, a recognition of this smallness rather than so much content and sweetness. I am not suggesting that

Esther should be given more 'opposition'—Saul Bellow's useful word—but that Dickens should conclude with some indication of his opposition since it has created so much in the whole world of the novel. Such opposition is included in some of the later novels.

Hard Times, Little Dorrit, A Tale of Two Cities, and *Great Expectations* make concluding demands on the reader which are appropriately limited and have no suggestion of expecting us to settle down and see everything and everyone as now likely to do nicely after all that pain. The sense of reality is something that starts at the beginnings of *Hard Times* with a certain toughening of the moral humours in the two chief women characters. Sissy Jupe is a more subdued type of the female heart than Esther, and we are moreover asked to concentrate not on Sissy but on Louisa who is exposed to experience not simply as a victim, like Esther Summerson, but as a susceptible and malleable human being who has a capacity for damnation.[1] Though the treatment of the working-class characters and industrial problems is sentimental, thin, and crass, the virtue of *Hard Times* lies in a new kind of truthfulness about social conditioning of character. We do not find the anatomy of destructiveness followed by a small-scale model of construction as in *Bleak House.* The humours of the self-made man *gloriosus,* in Bounderby, and of the convertible Utilitarian, in Gradgrind, are incisive and spirited, very much in the manner of those Jonsonian humours whose very narrowness produce a pressure of vitality. The presentation of the circus with its symbols of pastime, joy, and goodhearted sleaziness is effective

[1] See Chapter 3 for a full discussion of Louisa.

within the limits of the fable and, in spite of its em-
barrassing lisping innocence, responds adequately
enough to the counter-symbol of the fact-choked and
fact-choking schoolroom. The novel certainly lacks a
proper adult paradigm for the imaginative and sensual
life denied by Gradgrind, but so much of the focus is on
the child's education that this almost passes without
notice. That it does not pass quite without notice is
perhaps a tribute to the delineation of passion, repression, and conflict in Louisa. Dickens cannot really be
said to explore her inner life, but he manages very
skilfully, as he did with Dombey, to imply it.

Louisa does not go right down to the bottom of Mrs
Sparsit's imaged moral staircase, but her redemption is
treated with some sternness and there is no falsely
triumphant climax. The anatomy of a heartless education and a heartless industrialism, linked by the
criterion of efficiency, concludes with no more than a
sad and sober appraisal:

Herself again a wife—a mother—lovingly watchful of her
children, ever careful that they should have a childhood of the
mind no less than a childhood of the body, as knowing it to be
even a more beautiful thing, and a possession, any hoarded scrap
of which is a blessing and happiness to the wisest? Did Louisa
see this? Such a thing was never to be.

The last words to the Dear Reader, though discussing
the possibility of remedy, are free from optimistic flights:
'It rests with you and me, whether, in our two fields of
action, similar things shall be or not.' Dickens looks
forward to rebirth—in the lives of children still unborn
and in deathbed repentance—but he denies Louisa a

brave new life, and the quiet and almost matter-of-fact language makes a true and whole response to the experience of the novel. His delight in loud cheers and crescendos at the end is subdued, and he suggests that Louisa's future will be undertaken 'as part of no fantastic vow, or bond, or sisterhood ... but simply as a duty to be done'. It is particularly satisfying that Dickens avoids the pendulum-swing so grossly offensive in *Bleak House*, and does not move into the language and symbolism of strong feeling and vivid fancy in reaction to the world and values of hard fact. He matches heartless rationality with a rational warmth. The very last words of the novel are placed in the context of age and death, which controls the hopefulness: 'We shall sit with lighter bosoms on the hearth, to see the ashes of our fires turn grey and cold.' The image of grey ashes is wholly sensitive to the experience of Coketown, and admits its existence, in contrast to the way that Esther's little Bleak House depended on ignoring the larger bleakness.

Little Dorrit is a bigger and more complex venture than *Hard Times*, but the new sensibility and toughness remains and grows. Little Dorrit herself is no complex psychological study, but a very effective character who manages to be both symbolic and sufficiently a creature of time and place. She has a certain grotesqueness— a stuntedness and sexlessness—which helps both to stylize her character as an image of virtue and to make her a more natural prison-child. She is Dickens's most successfully heroic character since Oliver Twist. And she is helped by sharing the interest of the novel with Arthur Clennam, victim of another kind of imprisonment, and a character with more inner life than we have found up to now. He too is responsively and convincingly stunted by environment, and extricates himself slowly and exhaustedly. The virtue and energy Dickens celebrates in this novel is hard-won and battered. Here too the ending is triumphant only in a muted way, and has a rational sobriety and a lack of crescendo. Arthur and Little Dorrit, like Louisa, move into a 'modest' life. The last sentence of the novel, one of the most sensitive Dickens ever wrote, calls strongly on our sympathies but makes no attempt to wipe out our recollections of all that has happened. It is responsive to the restlessness, dissatisfactions, and irresoluteness that have marked so much of the action:

They went quickly down into the roaring streets, inseparable and blessed; and as they passed along in sunshine and shade, the noisy and the eager, and the arrogant and the forward and the vain, fretted and chafed, and made their usual uproar.

The whole novel is not written or imagined with such rational and complex control. There are flights of pity and ecstasy where Dickens is at his worst. When the Dorrit brothers die, for instance, Dickens has some excellent individual touches of act and feeling, in the account of the old man sending off his trinkets and clothing to be pawned, and some striking imagery for death: 'quietly, quietly, the lines of the plan of the great Castle melted'. But he moves off into the banalities of prayer—an act of feeling he simply cannot touch—and into a paradisal imagery which rings loud and hollow: 'The two brothers were before their Father; far beyond the twilight judgments of this world; high above its mists and obscurities.' Some of the appeals on behalf of Little Dorrit's frailty and goodness also fall into banality. I emphasize such sentimental patches because I do not want to imply that the late Dickens is entirely in control of himself, his characters and his readers. There is sentimentality, but it is not used to solve problems, reach conclusions and attempt a grandiose finality.

Little Dorrit is like *Bleak House* in its centripetal symbolism. The novelist draws our attention at almost every point to the insistent symbol of imprisonment. When we have mentioned the dark stench of the French prison, with dazzling light outside, and its microcosmic image of class and power, the travellers in quarantine, talking explicitly of prison, the Marshalsea, Dorrit's conceit of the grand European tour which is so like imprisonment, the blatant but striking comparison of the St Bernard hostel to a prison, Mrs Clennam's room and repressive religion, we have made no observations which the novelist does not make repeatedly and clearly for us. The scene has widened: England was like a Bleak House, human life and civilization is like a prison. Perhaps the sensuous life of the symbolism in *Bleak House* is missing here. The prison symbolism is more thinly intellectual, more obviously worked-out in simple equations, though it has a dimension of feeling, perhaps shown most vividly in the depression and restricted energies of Clennam, a prisoner almost incapable of stretching and moving into life. There is the disadvantage that Dickens, like Henry James, makes the characters themselves do so much of the symbol-making, and this is not only an increase

18

in tiring explicitness but at times less than plausible.

The most successful piece of institutional animation has nothing to do with the prison, but presents the Civil Service, then the citadel of ease and privilege, unassailed by competition, as the Circumlocution Office. Dickens creates a devastating analysis out of lengthy exposition—by now he could risk making speeches in the novels—and very funny satirical portraiture. The Tite Barnacle family is animated by ludicrous satire which rests on the solid basis of Dickens's introductory exegesis unfolding 'The Whole Science of Government'. After eleven paragraphs of expository satire Dickens feels free to use ridicule:

> He had a superior eye-glass dangling round his neck, but unfortunately had such flat orbits to his eyes, and such limp little eyelids, that it wouldn't stick in when he put it up, but kept tumbling out against his waistcoat buttons with a click that discomposed him very much.

The eyeglass and the limp little eyelids are part of the caricature of the affectation and feebleness of this ruling class, but there is the superfluous flight so dear to Dickens in the flat orbits of the eyes. The language has an accurate imitation of vagueness and polite exclamatoriness—many 'I says' and 'Look heres'—which are ludicrously punctuated by the business with the clicking eyeglass. Light comedy is certainly not an end in itself, and indeed the very lightness here is appropriate to the portraiture. The Tite Barnacles ought not to be so flimsy and silly, ought not to be figures of Dickensian fun. The levity is part of reproach and bitter criticism, but it is also typical of *Little Dorrit*'s less tense, grim, and enclosed satiric world. It would be hard to imagine Flora Finching and Mr F's Aunt, for instance, in *Bleak House*.

But as in *Bleak House* the comic is often neighbour to the grim or pathetic feeling. In *Bleak House* we pass innocently from chat about tainted chops to the grisly scene of Spontaneous Combustion. In these last novels Dickens seems to be able to contaminate one feeling by another, so that we scarcely know whether to call the fun grisly or the horror the more macabre for the presence of laughter. Dickens's imagination was always attracted by rich mixtures of feeling, and the mixtures grow richer in the late novels. The suicide of Merdle, the financier whose soiled name, taken from *merde*, gives him away, is preluded by some light comedy of manners in Fanny's drawing-room. It must be remembered that Fanny is a recent graduate from prison:

'I thought I'd give you a call, you know.'

'Charmed, I am sure,' said Fanny.

'So I am off,' added Mr Merdle, getting up. 'Could you lend me a penknife?'

It was an odd thing, Fanny, smilingly observed, for her who could seldom prevail upon herself even to write a letter, to lend to a man of such vast business as Mr Merdle. 'Isn't it?' Mr Merdle acquiesced; 'But I want one; and I know you have got several little wedding keepsakes about, with scissors and tweezers and such things in them. You shall have it back tomorrow.'

'Edmund' said Mrs Sparkler, 'open (now, very carefully, I beg and beseech, for you are so very awkward) the mother-of-pearl box on my little table there, and give Mr Merdle the mother-of-pearl penknife.'

'Thank you,' said Mr Merdle; 'but if you have got one with

a darker handle, I think I should prefer one with a darker handle.'

'Tortoise-shell?'

'Thank you', said Mr Merdle; 'yes. I think I should prefer tortoise-shell.'

Undertaking not to get ink on the knife, he goes off to kill himself.

One of the great successes of *Great Expectations* is its fusion of the individual story with the social indictment. Dickens shows in Pip the natural unconditioned life of the heart and the socially destructive process which weakens and distorts it, transforming instinct into calculation, human love into manipulation, generosity into greed, spontaneity into shame and ambition. Though it softens and sentimentalizes the class-issue by the pastoral image of Joe and his forge which begs the whole question of determinism, it does produce some striking criticisms and ironies. The human centre is socially expressive. Pip's aspirations as he climbs to the top are endowed by the tainted money typical of his society, but the process and some of the social and emotional changes involved are still relevant as the meritocracy rises. Both Joe and Biddy are fairly free of patronizing presentation, have dignity and toughness, are not babies like Sleary, but inhabit the adult world. The end originally planned by Dickens would have kept Estella and Pip apart, though even this version implies a certain optimism in Pip's ability to break with his social conditioning and start again, with the far from slight advantage of a good bourgeois education. But both the old and the revised endings show the modesty and lack of exclamatory climax of *Hard*

21

Times and *Little Dorrit*: Pip and Estella are sad and scarred people, and the last words of the book remind us of darkness as well as light. Dickens simplifies the social issues, certainly, but the indictment remains, and what optimism we find cannot be called facile.

Our Mutual Friend is also a conversion story with social significance. It too deals with class, wealth, and social mobility. Plot and moral action are tightly bound together, in a multiple action which takes us back to *Bleak House* and *Little Dorrit*. Like *Great Expectations*, it concerns a moral ordeal and test, though in this novel the test is set by the characters. The plot-makers within the novel are not frustrated, or perverse or innocent, and they come out as rather flat, like Harmon Rokesmith, or as cosy caricatures, like the Boffins. Harmon stages the pseudo-conversion of Boffin, the Golden Dustman whose heart of gold becomes— Midas-like—chilled and hardened. This impersonated corruption acts as a test and a warning to Bella Wilfer, a nice girl with mercenary leanings. The false conversion brings about the true one. In this novel Dickens separates the subjects of money and class, dealing with them in different actions, though there is plenty of linking material in the chorus of Veneerings and Podsnaps. The story of Bella and the Boffins might have involved class but is simply a fable about love and money, while the story of Lizzie Harmon and her rival lovers deals expressly with problems of class, aspiration, conflict, and division. Bradley Headstone, the repressed, respectable, and passionate school-master is opposed to Eugene Wrayburn, the idle, *ennuyé*, able, and perverse gentleman. Backed by Charlie, Lizzie's clever and ambitious brother, these characters act out a splendid *crime passionel* which is thickly detailed and documented as socially determined action.

The several mysteries, some overt, some covert, are less concentratedly unified than the action of *Bleak House*: there is the impersonation of Rokesmith by Harmon, which goes back to *Martin Chuzzlewit*, the impersonation of a miser by Boffin, the story of the crime, and rich supporting material, grotesque, comic, pathetic, and satiric. The best thing in the novel is the psychological study of crime, not exactly new in Dickens, who had long ago shown Sikes's solitude and guilt and fear in the fire and listening to the cheapjack selling stain-remover, then a little later, Jonas Chuzzlewit and his telltale heart, but new in its careful sociological backing. In the analysis of Bradley he moves out of the so-called 'criminal classes' to draw a new kind of meritocratic monster whose violence, repression, and jealousy are part of a deadly struggle for respectability and sexuality in a not very intelligent man of strong passions and a need for social conformity. Dickens's method seems deceptively simple, tending to sociopsychological analysis on the one hand, and expressive stage-gestures like the beating of a hand on a stone, on the other. But what is admirable and very far from simple is the coherence of thriller and social criticism, fused with that control of contrary feelings which created the scene with the tortoise-shell penknife. In the discovery scene in Bradley's schoolroom, for instance, Rogue Riderhood comes in the grimly ridiculous guise of a friendly visitor wanting to put the children through their paces. The well-drilled chorus

23

of children chirping their facts speaks fully for the education which has shaped Bradley, and provides just the right kind of thin surface of innocent routine on which Riderhood can threateningly play and then violently break through, after a tensely mounting examination not unlike his namesake Red Ridinghood's interrogation of the wolf.

But the novel as a whole lacks the control and unity of such individual scenes. Despite the story of crime and punishment, the character of Wrayburn, and the excellent comedy of Wegg and Venus, a pair of bizarre, Morality grotesques, there is much flat and un-developed action, softness of character, and an un-satisfactory relation between the whole and its parts. Wrayburn marries Lizzie, perhaps reflecting a new flexibility in social attitudes to marriage between the classes, as Humphry House in *The Dickens World* (London, 1941) suggests, though with crucial stages in his conflict and decision blurred by grave illness, and a symbolic rescue from death and the river. His marriage is finally approved by Twemlow, a choric character of some importance, a 'real' gentleman amongst the *nouveaux riches*, and an interesting new stereotype created by Dickens, the *gentleman* with a heart of gold. Although the novel is bristling with convincing social victims like Charley Hexam and Bradley, its converted or virtuous characters are very much less appropriately convincing. Dickens's densely documented analysis of Bradley only shows up the dreaminess of such figures as Bella and the Boffins, and even Eugene has to be helped over the tricky area of decision by symbolic action. The striking and impressive figures of the Podsnaps, the Lammles, and the Veneerings, act out their own little drama and thus become much more than a comic chorus, creating a satiric action which is much closer to Thackeray's powerful caricature of a whole world, in *Vanity Fair*, than anything else in Dickens. If *Bleak House* moves us through pity and disgust, and *Little Dorrit* through ironic claustrophobia, *Our Mutual Friend* moves us through the sharpest and most strident satire Dickens ever created. It is the satire which appears on the margin of previous novels but which, to my mind, takes over in this novel and creates a world in which the benevolent softnesses of Mr Wilfer the Cherub and Bella's baby and Wrayburn's marriage and little Johnny's words in the Children's Hospital about 'the boofer lady', simply shrivel up before our eyes. The best that we can find in this world is the likely alliance of the Lammles, taken in and making the best of things, or of Jenny Wren, with her sustaining fantasy of the father who is a child.

Dickens creates such a powerful anatomy of a corrupting and corrupted society, ruled and moved by greed and ambition, that the wish-fulfilling fantasies of virtue and conversion are too fragile to support faith. That contemptuous insight out of which he drew Podsnap's humours and the grotesque dust-heaps where the scavenging Wegg prods with his wooden leg is realized in the concreteness of sensuous detail and appropriate language. Dickens can make virtue lisp like a baby or rhapsodize like a saint, but it seldom speaks with the unerring individual tones of Podsnap's loud patronizing complacency or the drunken ellipses

25

of Dolls or the soaring tones of moral grandeur of the Lammles' duet. Virtue often speaks in the neutral language that expresses neither personality nor class, as in Mrs Boffin or Lizzie, where style is not only dead but also glosses over the social difficulties of her love and marriage. Boffin the miser is so much more sharply incised in manners and speech—'Scrunch or be scrunched'—than Boffin the good old man, that it is not surprising that Gissing thought Dickens must have really intended to make the Golden Dustman a study in deterioration. Betty Higden is endowed with a certain life because she is given a language, and she is perhaps the most effective instance of virtuous energy in the book. The others are either nonentities or unappealing: Bella does not want to be the doll in the doll's house, but her marriage and maternity are nothing if not embarrassingly doll-like. Neither the action nor the psychology of individual goodness is strong enough to heal those sore spots shown and painfully touched in pity and violence and satire. But the ending expands beyond the doll's house, and, as T. A. Jackson pointed out, there is no simple moral triumph here, but the survival of the Veneerings and the Podsnaps. There is duality, but no complacency or reduction.

2 The Change of Heart (1)

Moral conversion lies at the heart of many novels. And we might use William James's distinction between the sudden conversion, or *crisis*, of St Paul, and the gradual conversion, or *lysis*, of Bunyan or Tolstoy, to distinguish between *Robinson Crusoe* and *Martin Chuzzlewit*, novels of abrupt change, and *Emma*, *Daniel Deronda*, and *The Ambassadors*, chronicles of gradual progress. Although Dickens must be classed with Defoe, in structure and psychology, as a novelist of *crisis*, the moral implications of his novels place him with Jane Austen, George Eliot, and Henry James. Robinson Crusoe, on the Island of Despair, is converted by storm, sickness, and vision, to a faith in his guiding Providence, and his material rewards are considerable. Both Providence and material success are tainted concepts for Dickens, George Eliot, and Meredith, and the typical conversion of the great Victorian novel is not a religious conversion but a turning from self-regard to love and social responsibility. A crude graph of Dickens's typical treatment of moral progress would also bring him close to George Eliot and James. In all three novelists (and in others) the hero is converted by seeing and understanding his defect and its origins. Insight and fairly explicit revaluation set him free for a fresh start. All three seem to be using their art to qualify a belief in determinism by a belief in freedom: environment, heredity, and chance combine to make conversion necessary, but individuals are given the insight and power to re-make themselves. But the hero is not isolated as a typical heroic figure. He is controlled by social and moral variations which emphasize the power of environment and the difficulty of change: we observe Pecksniff and Jonas Chuzzlewit, as well as Martin; Bulstrode and Lydgate, as well as Dorothea; Chad and Waymarsh and Jim Pocock, as well as Strether. But the fundamental concept of possible conversion, even in the muted forms of *Middlemarch*, rests on an optimistic belief in will and intelligence. An important feature in all these delineations of moral change is the hero's ability to recognize and formulate his own limitations.

The variations are of course considerable, and this kind of rough general summary looks inadequate when challenged by the rich variety of actual cases. No formula can do justice to a form which includes the comic education of Emma's sense and sensibility; the frustrated triumphs of Dorothea's painfully acquired faith and realism; and Strether's slow and complex rejection, in a middle-aged *Bildungsroman*, of the materialism and puritanism of Woollett and the pure aesthetic sense of Paris. All these portrayals of change are complete and continuous moral actions, accreted in a close imitation of persons, events, social habits, and slow time. The theme of conversion is co-extensive with the whole form of the narrative, and the optimistic suggestion of moral progress is part of a fine elaborate mesh of cause and effect. Dickens's optimism may look cruder than George Eliot's because of the absence of this

28

fine mesh. His imitation of persons is conveyed in a stereotyped, not a realistically complex, psychology, and his conversions often depend on a theatrical telescoping of time. Nor is the subject of moral change his exclusive interest: at his weakest, in *Martin Chuzzle-wit*, the moral change is virtually insulated from the main flow of action, not just because it is separated in place, but because Martin's early selfishness and his later unselfishness are trivially substantiated and have little influence on the action. Even at his best, with the progress of David Copperfield or Pip, Dickens never endows a character with that imaginative sensibility and energy which gives weight and truth to the progress of Gwendolen Harleth, Isabel Archer, or Harry Richmond. Allowing for such major differences, it is still possible to recognize that although Dickens's mode of presentation, for many reasons, depends on fantasy rather than realism, his changing characters have something in common with the changing characters of George Eliot and James. Scrooge, Pip, and Bella Wilfer pass through some of the same stages of vision and revision as Emma, Gwendolen, and Strether.

Sudden conversion has a long history, in the drama and the novel. In Elizabethan and Jacobean drama (in Greene, Shakespeare, Jonson, and Tourneur, for instance) it often comes as a convenient final reconciliation. Surprisingly, perhaps, it seldom has this kind of concluding function in Dickens, though it sometimes has in Wilkie Collins. Dickens never shows us a Moll Flanders. He does, it is true, convert Micawber from Micawberism, and he does unite Dombey and Florence, but neither conversion comes as a surprising

29

flourish when the illusion is wearing thin and the need for plausible demonstration has disappeared. The change in both Micawber and Dombey is prepared. Micawber's administrative apotheosis follows his energetic triumph over Heep, and the possible implausibility of his actions is decorously covered by the transitional mystery of his changed behaviour to Mrs Micawber and David. Besides, there have been earlier triumphs of efficiency, like his masterly salvaging of David's disastrous dinner-party. Dombey is a more serious character and a more serious case of change, but in *Novels of the Eighteen Forties* (London, 1958) Kathleen Tillotson has shown convincingly that this is not a case of abrupt change: Dombey's sensibility, silences, and his extravagant commitment to cruelty, as Dickens himself pointed out in reply to the charge of violent change, reveal his unspoken conflict. There are occasional small conversions, like Tom Gradgrind's deathbed repentance, but they are not conspicuous. The kind of conversion I have in mind, however, does not usually conclude the novel; it is rather the moral change on which action hinges, or appears to hinge.

The change of heart may provide the chief interest of the story, as in *A Christmas Carol*, a large part of the interest, as in *Great Expectations* and *Our Mutual Friend*, or a relatively unsubstantial part, as in *Martin Chuzzlewit*. It may play an apparently small part, as in Tattycoram's conversion in *Little Dorrit*, but illuminate much more than its immediate area of action. It may be presented in terms of strict *Bildungsroman*, as part of the process of growing up, as in *David Copperfield*, or it

30

may be the crisis of an ironically retarded education, as in *Hard Times*. All these examples of the change of heart have one thing in common: where George Eliot and James transcribe the moral process in slow motion and loving detail, allowing for its irregular pulse, its eddy, its wayward lapse and false start, Dickens shows it as quick, simple, and settled. The converted hero never looks back: not for Martin Chuzzlewit the lapses of Fred Vincy, not for David Copperfield Strether's discovery that the new value, like the old, may have to be revised. George Eliot and James show moral change as an accumulation of many actions and reactions, as a continuous process. Dickens's conversions are startlingly rapid in comparison, though not always as rapid as his own chosen convention makes them seem.

This chosen convention depends on the moral double or opposite. The hero is changed by seeing his situation or his moral defect enacted for him in external coincidence: by his twin, who forces a recognition of loathsome resemblance, or his opposite, who forces reluctant admiration and comparison. He sees his defect enlarged, isolated, unmistakably his own, but detached for inspection. And he acts on this recognition, and is irrevocably changed. The situation is crystallized and the double acts as devil's advocate, as in Stevenson's *Markheim* or Kipling's *Drama of Duncan Parrenness*, or as model and guide, like Poe's *William Wilson*. Many examples of doubles are discussed by Ralph Tymms in *Doubles in Literary Psychology* (Cambridge, 1949), but as his interest is confined to the double in the literal sense, he glances briefly at the Brothers Cheeryble, and at Darnay and Carton, and dismisses Dickens's use of

31

the double as insignificant, typical of 'the non-psychological approach of the time'. This is hard on Dickens. His doubles are moral, seldom physical, but their role is often identical with the role of the double in Chamisso's 'Erscheinung', which Professor Tymms notes as a good example of the *Seelenspiegel* or soul-mirror[1]. The double who has this converting role has little of the symbolic ambiguity of Conrad and Dostoevsky: he appears as part of the realistic action, as a substantial character involved in personal, as well as moral, relations with the hero. Dickens's satirical habit of diffusing examples of specialized vices and virtues throughout the novel (from *Martin Chuzzlewit* onwards) may deflect our interest from this role. The novels are full of twins and opposites, but in the crisis of conversion the mirror is offered to the character, in effective mime and therapy, as well as to the reader, in irony and generalization. The mime is simple, but its implications are many.

The example which will come to everyone's mind is the only example where an actual physical double is used to play a part in moral change. Lauriat Lane describes the twinship of Darnay and Carton, in *A Tale of Two Cities*, as a device which allows Dickens to bring about the perfect wish-fulfilment of sacrifice and happy ending. This is not the whole story. It is significant that when Sidney Carton first sees Darnay, he performs a good act, using the striking resemblance to break down

[1] Lauriat Lane, in 'Dickens and the Double' *The Dickensian*, lv (1959), 47–55, goes to the other extreme, and far from confining himself to literal doubles, spends much of his time in exploring suggestions of the *alter ego* in the portraits of Jonas Chuzzlewit and John Jasper—in the latter case speculating freely. His interest lies in possible traces of a split-personality in Dicken's criminal psychology, and he is not concerned with the converting *Seelenspiegel*.

the witness who is identifying Darnay, and saving his double for the first time. When he draws the court's attention to the resemblance, it is strong, but a few minutes later the 'momentary earnestness' disappears, giving away to this usual reckless and disreputable look, so that some of the onlookers 'said to one another they would hardly have thought the two were so alike'. When Carton takes his 'counterpart' to dine, he rejects both resemblance and affinity, saying, 'Don't let your sober face elate you, however; you don't know what it may come to'. After they part, Carton looks at his face in the mirror, seeing himself, as Darnay has seen him, as a 'Double of coarse deportment' and then making this explicit recognition:

'Do you particularly like the man?' he muttered, at his own image; 'why should you particularly like a man who resembles you? There is nothing in you to like; you know that. Ah, confound you! What a change you have made in yourself! A good reason for taking to a man, that he shows you what you have fallen away from, and what you might have been!' (ch. iv)

This doubling is an important part of the plot, bringing about the special irony when Darnay and Carton both fall in love with Lucie, and eventually enabling Carton to sacrifice himself for Darnay and redeem his wasted possibilities. (It takes a character in George Eliot, Mirah in *Daniel Deronda*, to comment on the emotional luxury of such an act.) But Carton is redeemed by the love of a good woman, not just by this image of what might have been. He tells Lucie that all his life 'might have been' and she says, anticipating and inspiring his death, 'I am sure that the best part of it might still be'.

33

It takes more (or less) than love to redeem Martin Chuzzlewit and Pip.

Love is relevant, however, to the discussion of Scrooge. Because this is the only example of an entirely fantastic treatment of conversion I should like to depart from chronology, and begin my illustration of this recurring convention with *A Christmas Carol*. Marley's ghost wrings his chained hands as he contemplates the moral plight of Scrooge, and laments: 'Why did I walk through the crowds of fellow beings with my eyes turned down, and never raise them to that Blessed Star which led the Wise men to a poor abode!' (Stave 1). Scrooge, like many another Victorian anti-hero, is the Utilitarian Wise Man, and he is forced to find the poor abode and forced to give. Before he can lift his eyes to the Star he has first to turn them on himself. Like all Dickens's Utilitarian egoists, he needs to have his heart taken by storm, and the storm comes in the shape of nostalgia, pity, and fear. Humphry House calls it 'crude magic of reformation' but this might be qualified.

Scrooge sees his own image in the most literal fashion, moving back in time and confronting himself at different stages in his process of deterioration. There is his old self, the child, loving and innocent opposite of the unloving old sophist. There is the transitional self, committed to loveless rationalism, but still holding some few warm contacts with the past. There is his mirror-image, the present self who echoes his own words and sentiments but in a context newly charged with feeling. The doubles, like the ghosts, are all potent in different ways, and indeed the ghosts are not only aspects of

34

Christmas but in part at least aspects of Scrooge: his past, his present, and his suggestively anonymous future. The return to childhood restores him to the first springs of love in a way reminiscent of Wordsworth and George Eliot; the personal past is a tradition which can keep alive the feeling child, father of the rational man. It also gives a brief glimpse at the deprived and isolated child. Instead of a recognition of causality—though I think that is obliquely present for the reader—we have in Scrooge himself the equally effective stirring of love and pity. He sees his sister, rather as Silas Marner remembers his sister after he first sees Eppie, and the link is made with old affection and old sorrow. He 'feels pity for his former self' and the pity brings with it the first movement of imaginative self-criticism. He identifies his old sorrow with sorrow outside himself: 'There was a boy singing a Christmas Carol at my door last night. I should like to have given him something: that's all' (Stave II). This is of course the carol which gives the story its name, and also its theme: 'God bless you, merry gentlemen, May nothing you dismay.' Scrooge threatens the boy with his ruler, rejects the blessing, and Christmas brings him a strong but salutary dismay.

The Ghost of Christmas Past acts as devil's advocate, and his timing is admirable. Scrooge is identifying himself with his former self at Fezziwig's ball: 'His heart and soul were in the scene, and with his former self. He corroborated everything, remembered everything, enjoyed everything, and underwent the strangest agitation' (Stave II). The Ghost pours cold water on the apprentices' gratitude: 'A small matter ... to make these silly folks so full of gratitude ... He has spent but a few pounds of your mortal money: three or four perhaps.' So Scrooge is forced to defend the generous spirit, 'heated by the remark, and speaking unconsciously like his former, not his latter, self: "The happiness he gives, is quite as great as if it cost a fortune".' Then he suddenly remembers his present self, and gently urged by his ghostly analyst, moves towards self-criticism. The process is continued by the second Ghost, in Stave III, who answers Scrooge's anxious question about Tiny Tim: 'If he be like to die, he had better do it, and decrease the surplus population.' When Scrooge is overcome 'with penitence and grief' at his own words, the Ghost comes in quickly with the grave rebuke: 'forbear that wicked cant until you have discovered What the surplus is, and Where it is.' The Ghost employs the same mimicry when he shows the terrible children, Want and Ignorance. Scrooge's newborn horror, like his compassion, is answered by his own words: 'Are there no prisons? ... Are there no workhouses?' This technique of exact quotation comes decorously enough in the Christmas present, rubbing Scrooge's nose in his very recent refusal to give to the portly gentleman. The arguments for charity were also presented in personification ('Want is keenly felt, and Abundance rejoices') but they have to be acted out for the unimaginative man, forcing him to walk through the crowds and see them composed not of ciphers but of individuals. All the elements in this brief masque are appropriate. They show the hardened man the need and love in his own past; they show the old killjoy his dead capacity for joy. Having indicated causality and change the show ends with a *memento mori*, cold, solitary, and repulsive, in the new perspective of feeling. Effective argument is implied in the dramatic reclamation by love and fear, and we are left with the urgent question —is reclamation still possible?—which makes the modulation from nightmare to reality. The fantasy has a realistic suggestion of hynotic therapy.

But the content is supernatural and the effects greatly foreshortened. The process of conversion is everywhere else in Dickens transferred to a rather more realistic mode. Martin Chuzzlewit's conversion, for example, is as traumatic as that of Scrooge. It comes with a violent and unreal change of environment, Pavlovian in kind and effect, after Martin's sickness and his disillusion with Eden. The mode of external moral enactment is very close to the masque of *A Christmas Carol*, though it is Mark Tapley, the double as opposite, who provides the mirror. Mark has been nursing Martin, then the roles are reversed, and it is 'Martin's turn to work, and sit beside the bed and watch'. Mark keeps on crying brightly, 'I'm jolly, sir: I'm jolly!' and Martin's un-imaginative egoism is jolted by the similarity and the difference in the two situations. The running title is 'The Discovery of Self':

Now, when Martin began to think of this, and to look at Mark as he lay there; never reproaching him by so much as an expression of regret ... he began to think, how was it that this man who had had so few advantages, was so much better than he who had had so many? ... he began to ask himself in what they differed.

He was assisted in coming to a conclusion on this head by the frequent presence of Mark's friend, their fellow-passenger across the ocean: which suggested to him that in regard to having aided her, for example, they had differed very much. Somehow he coupled Tom Pinch with this train of reflection; and thinking that Tom would be very likely to have struck up the same sort of acquaintance under similar circumstances, began to think in what respects two people so extremely different were like each other, and were unlike him. At first sight there was nothing very distressing in these meditations, but they did undoubtedly distress him for all that. (ch. xxxiii)

The reader has of course anticipated Martin's groping classification, but the obvious bracketing of Mark Tapley and Tom Pinch is an important moment of insight for a character so far placed firmly in the egoists' category. Dickens's organization of doubles and opposites seems a simple formal device for giving clarity to narrative and theme, but artifice and morality interact with each other just as they do in more subtle novelists where psychological realism and particularity blur the categories. Even here the form is in part the result of a way of looking at life, and the moment of conversion largely depends on the way in which the character catches up with the reader and becomes aware of the categories in which he is himself placed. In this moral crisis Martin's recognition precedes his movement from one category to another, and both recognition and change are made very self-conscious processes. But there follows immediately one of Dickens's quiet authorial comments. He takes a look at the origin of Martin's humour, as he has indeed done much earlier in the novel when Martin explains to Tom that he has been brought up by his 'abominably selfish' grandfather, whose failings—family failings, he has heard—have

38

fortunately not descended to him. Dickens here gives the detached explanation. Selfishness, he says, was the domestic vice propagated by Martin's grandfather, and Martin had acquired a defensive selfishness, reasoning, as a child, 'My guardian takes so much thought for himself, that unless I do the like by *myself*, I shall be forgotten.' This is a relatively cursory glance at causality, but it is made. Dickens then comments truly that Martin had never known his fault:

> If any one had taxed him with the vice, he would have indignantly repelled the accusation, and conceived himself unworthily aspersed. He never would have known it, but that being newly risen from a bed of dangerous sickness, to watch by such another couch, he felt how nearly Self had dropped into the grave, and what a poor dependent, miserable thing it was.
>
> It was natural for him to reflect—he had months to do it in—upon his own escape, and Mark's extremity. This led him to consider which of them could be better spared, and why? Then the curtain slowly rose a very little way; and Self, Self, Self, was shown below.

The discovery that his essential self is selfish (Dickens plays with the double meaning) is tactfully described in this image of the slow curtain. Dickens describes the process of change so briefly—making no attempt to give any correlative for the passage of time—that even though he says that the process took months, we are left with the implausible impression of violent change. Dickens is in fact *saying*, but not *showing*, that this is no single leap of vision but a slow and complex process:

> It was long before he fixed the knowledge of himself so firmly in his mind that he could thoroughly discern the truth; but in the

hideous solitude of that most hideous place, with Hope so far removed, Ambition quenched, and Death beside him rattling at the very door, reflection came, as in a plague-beleaguered town; and so he felt and knew the failing of his life, and saw distinctly what an ugly spot it was.

Eden has been the reverse of hope and illusion and pride, but by a further irony Martin's process reverses the Fall, for 'So low had Eden brought him down. So high had Eden raised him up.' Here are the elements of Scrooge's reclamation: insight is painfully born from a detached and clear reflection, and there is a similar context of panic, horror, and death. Even the masque is shadowed in the strong personifications of Hope, Ambition, Death, and the plague-beleaguered town, which is both a metaphor and a real place.

Martin's conversion is much slower than Scrooge's immediate and successful transformation, but although Dickens says it is slow, it is shown in a way which gives no impression of the real pace. Dickens is very often showing moral development in narrative *cul-de-sac*, not equating the main action of the novel with the action of change. In *David Copperfield* there is rather less of a gap between the flow of events and the moral action. The nature of the moral change has been discussed by Gwendolyn Needham, who points out that for David the moment of insight comes when he hears Annie Strong tell of 'the first impulse of an undisciplined heart' and 'love founded on a rock' ('The Undisciplined Heart of David Copperfield', *Nineteenth Century Fiction*, ix (1954), 81–107). Her words strike home because they both duplicate and reverse his situation: she has felt the first impulse but not followed it. Insight does not come all at once, and when David first hears Annie's words about disparity of mind and purpose, we are told, 'I pondered on those words, even while I was studiously attending to what followed, as if they had some particular interest, or some strange application that I could not divine' (ch. xlv). Her comment on the undisciplined heart is spoken 'with an earnestness that thrilled'. Then at the end of a chapter David cannot attend to his aunt's words:

I was thinking of all that had been said. My mind was still running on some of the expressions used. 'There can be no disparity in marriage like unsuitability of mind and purpose.' 'My love was founded on a rock.' But we were at home; and the trodden leaves were lying underfoot, and the autumn wind was blowing.

We reach something approaching explicitness in the pathetic tone and associations—the 'too late'—of the natural images, but David's divination still lags a little behind the reader's. It is not until three chapters later, after we have been shown yet another mirror in the story of Betsy Trotwood's undisciplined heart, and after we have seen David trying hard to correct Dora's 'disparity', that we are told how full recognition has pervaded his life with 'the old unhappy feeling':

'The first mistaken impulse of an undisciplined heart.' Those words of Mrs Strong's were constantly recurring to me, at this time; were almost always present to my mind. I awoke with them, often, in the night; I remember to have even read them, in dreams, inscribed upon the walls of houses. For I knew, now, that my own heart was undisciplined when it first loved Dora; and that if it had been disciplined, it could never have felt, when we were married, what it had felt in its secret experience.

'There can be no disparity in marriage, like unsuitability of

41

mind and purpose.' These words I remembered too. I had endeavoured to adapt Dora to myself, and found it impracticable. It remained for me to adapt myself to Dora ... This was the discipline to which I tried to bring my heart, when I began to think. (ch. xlviii)

The moment of insight is again spread out in time, though condensed for the reader into one memorable scene. David does not leap into action, but accepts trial and error and bewilderment. Once more the character is made aware of the moral categories which shape the novel, and by the end we see that Annie Strong's situation, which first applied only in part to David's, is the complete parallel: for David, as for Annie and Peggotty, it is the heart's discipline which founds love on a rock. We might once more point to a discrepancy between the narrative action and the moral development: David's process is only briefly one of discipline, and then the artist's wish-fulfilment disposes of Dora and what remains is less a stern moral test than the slow discovery that Agnes is the rock on which he should found his love. He is blind ('blind! blind! blind!') to his dependence on her rather than to a weakness which life harshly corrects. But this is not the place to discuss all the implications of Dickens's morality: whatever the nature of the moral conversion, it is once more made, with brevity and insight, by this dramatic enactment outside the hero's consciousness.

Gradgrind, in *Hard Times*, is also converted by two images, his double and his opposite, made available by the usual pattern of moral stereotypes. The two are not combined, as they are for David, but split, as they are for Scrooge. Gradgrind's redeeming opposite is

42

Sissy, the pupil who teaches her master that the truth of the heart can be stronger than the truth of the reason, and he can learn her lesson only when faced by the sterile fruits of his teaching in another pupil, his daughter. Then comes the moment of insight which is here partly retrospective, for he sees that 'some change may have been slowly working about me in this house, by mere love and gratitude'. But his double is as effective a master as the model, and more ironical. Full insight comes like Nemesis when he too is quoted out of his own mouth. His dishonest son says,

So many people are employed in conditions of trust; so many people, out of so many, will be dishonest. I have heard you talk, a hundred times, of its being a law. How can *I* help laws? You have comforted others with such things, father. Comfort yourself. (bk. III, ch. vii)

The statistical unit confounds the statistician, and Tom is made even more detestable and ridiculous by the 'disgraceful grotesqueness' of his comic minstrel disguise. The truth is driven home in the form of gross parody.

But there are three successful pupils who act as double. His son's parody is followed by a re-enactment of the past. The question-and-answer of the first school-room scene is reversed when the perfect pupil of Utilitarianism gives the text-book answer: ' "Bitzer," said Mr Gradgrind, broken down, and miserably submissive to him, "have you a heart?" "The circulation, sir," returned Bitzer, smiling at the oddity of the question, "couldn't be carried on without one" ' (bk. III, ch. viii). The new Gradgrind goes on speaking of ordinary human values to Bitzer, going innocently

43

against the established grain of his own system, arguing pathetically, 'If this is solely a matter of self-interest with you' and 'You were many years at my school'. In his need he sees not only that his precepts are dust, but that they have hardened in the malice of Bitzer's rational replies. His last instruction comes from the world of the circus and its idle frivolity, making its point in comic lisp: 'There ith a love in the world, not Thelf-interetht after all.' At the end Gradgrind is far from his sophisticated pupils, and learns truth from dogs and clowns.

There is a small and very characteristic example in *Little Dorrit* which shows all the constituents of this kind of moral crisis. Miss Wade first seduces Tattycoram by fanning her jealousy. She sees herself as she watches Tattycoram's fit of fury and 'ingratitude', and it is hard not to feel that this is one of Dickens's smug diagnoses: 'The observer stood with her hand upon her own bosom, looking at the girl, as one afflicted with a diseased part might curiously watch the dissection and exposition of an analogous case' (bk. 1, ch. ii). And Tattycoram has just said to her, 'You seem to come like my own anger, my own malice ...' Miss Wade captures the analogous case, and tries to avenge herself by exacerbating Tattycoram's less unredeemable jealousy and resentment. It is rather like a Morality abstraction influencing a more realistic mixed character, and the result is a good example of the moral homeopathy I have been illustrating, for the jealousy is purged not increased. Tattycoram explains:

I was afraid of her, from the first time I ever saw her. I knew she had got a power over me, through understanding what was bad in me, so well. It was a madness in me, and she could raise it whenever she liked. I used to think, when I got into that state, that people were all against me because of my first beginning; and the kinder they were to me, the worse fault I found in them. I made it out that they triumphed above me, and that they wanted to make me envy them, when I know—when I even knew then, if I would—that they never thought of such a thing ... I am not so bad as I was ... I have had Miss Wade before me all this time, as if it were my own self grown ripe— turning everything the wrong way, and twisting all good into evil. I have had her before me all this time, finding no pleasure in anything but keeping me as miserable, suspicious, and tormenting as herself ... (bk. II, ch. xxxiii)

This is the purest example of conversion by double, and Tattycoram gives obliquely the perfect comment on the distortions of Miss Wade's autobiography. There is also of course the central figure of another waif, Little Dorrit, who comes in just after this speech. Tattycoram has been instructed by her own self grown ripe, a stronger devil who exorcizes her own, and now Mr Meagles tells her to regard her opposite, like Martin Chuzzlewit: 'If she had constantly thought of herself, and settled with herself that everybody visited this place upon her ... she would have led an irritable and probably a useless existence.' Tattycoram's story, like Miss Wade's, is an antithetical variant of Dorrit's, another study in the novel's exploration of conditioning and freedom.

Pip's progress in *Great Expectations* is probably the only instance of a moral action where the events precipitate change and growth as they do in George Eliot or Henry James. Pip is marked by a dominant flaw like Scrooge, but the flaw does not absorb the whole vitality of the character. He is a more realistic and analytical Martin Chuzzlewit and he is shown subjected to the influences of accident and environment, and hardening in his pride and ingratitude, though never without some measure of shame. The main converting event is his discovery of the source of his expectations, but this is a fairly complex business, involving the delicately handled shifting relationship with Magwitch. This is certainly not only a symbolic delineation of the criminal basis of wealth, though at times it carries that implication. Magwitch is also an important agent in the conversion of Pip. He first exacerbates and then exorcizes pride and ingratitude.

Pip's view of this nemesis is still steeped in his twin failings:

But sharpest and deepest pain of all—it was for the convict, guilty of I knew not what crimes, and liable to be taken out of those rooms where I sat thinking, and hanged at the Old Bailey door, that I had deserted Joe. (ch. xxxix)

Here he is merely revaluing one particular instance of pride and ingratitude, and what he has to learn, like all unimaginative men, is a generalized and renewable morality. He has to revalue his defects, not an isolated example of them. Magwitch plays a role in this Morality rather like that of King Grizzlybeard in the fairy tale, who degrades pride and gives it a real cause and a fitting punishment. Pip, like a spoilt child, is really given something to cry about. Pip has winced at Joe's illiteracy and manners, and so he is forced into the gross parody and ordeal of stomaching Magwitch, who

46

has paid for Pip's education and fastidiousness. Then Pip becomes involved in Magwitch's past and future, and Magwitch himself is given dignity and sympathy. Both he and Pip move out of aggressive pride into trust and love. Magwitch then provokes a further revaluation in Pip, based now on an appraisal of the convict's gratitude, and an acknowledgement of his own debt:

> When I took my place by Magwitch's side, I felt that was my place henceforth while he lived.
> For now my repugnance to him had all melted away, and in the hunted wounded shackled creature who held my hand in his, I only saw a man who had meant to be my benefactor, and who had felt affectionately, gratefully, and generously, towards me with great constancy through a series of years. I only saw in him a much better man than I had been to Joe. (ch. liv)

Magwitch draws out and punishes Pip's pride and ingratitude,[1] then delineates Pip for himself and the reader in his role as moral opposite. Lastly, he provides the final ordeal which proves Pip's conversion. Pip holds Magwitch's hand during the trial, and the spectators 'pointed down at this criminal or at that, and most of all at him and me' (ch. lvi).

Although Estella's relations with her benefactor largely parallel Pip's, her moral change takes place offstage, and it is Miss Havisham's conversion which corresponds to Pip's. She is like Miss Wade in strengthening her own ruling passion by encouraging it in someone else—a subtle form of self-justification and revenge. She of course propagates her lovelessness

[1] Although I cannot entirely accept Dorothy Van Ghent's view of the relationship in *The English Novel: Form and Function* (New York, 1953), the account is not irreconcilable with her interpretation.

47

in her education of Estella, and like Gradgrind she is punished at the hands of the pupil who has learnt only too well. Estella hears Pip's declaration of love unmoved, and explains, 'It is in the nature formed within me.' When Miss Havisham demands the one thing she has trained Estella not to give—'Would it be weakness to return my love?'—Estella can only ask:

> If you had taught her, from the dawn of her intelligence, with your utmost energy and might, that there was such a thing as daylight but that it was made to be her enemy and destroyer, and she must always turn against it, for it had blighted you and would else blight her;—if you had done this, and then, for a purpose, had wanted her to take naturally to the daylight and she could not do it, you would have been disappointed and angry? (ch. xxxviii)

Miss Havisham is taught by her self-created double, but the encounter shows her that she is in fact teaching lovelessness while desperately needing love. She sees her error in this distorting mirror. Then, like Scrooge, she sees her old self in the image of Pip. He provides this image of love just after she has been rebuffed by the image of lovelessness, and she tells Pip, after his rejection by Estella, 'Until you spoke to her the other day, and until I saw in you a looking-glass that showed me what I once felt myself, I did not know what I had done' (ch. xlix). There is no action left for her, but she admits responsibility, and knows that she has shut Estella, like herself, away from the influences that form 'the natural heart', that 'with this figure of myself always before her, a warning to back and point my lesson, I stole her heart away and put ice in its place'.

48

Estella comes to find that suffering is 'stronger than all other teaching' but that is a process not demonstrated in the novel.

There remains Dickens's last portrayal of conversion. The central moral crisis in *Our Mutual Friend*, the conversion of Bella from mercenariness to love, shows Dickens's precise awareness of this kind of moral therapy. For Boffin and his wife deliberately act out the homeopathic cure, staging her mercenary values and repelling her into the right course. It is Dickens's great surprise, as he tells us in the Epilogue, the card hidden up his sleeve from which our attention has carefully been averted by the deliberately flaunted impersonation by Harmon. Harmon himself, again like King Grizzly-beard, personates the poor man, and he and the Boffins collaborate in Bella's conversion. At the climax Boffin is both double and alter ego, for he assumes the miser's mask, most unlike his true self, and presents with verve the exaggerated and logically active image of Bella's supposed values. This releases the true forces of benevolence with a powerful spring. After the deceptive appearance of the good man perverted by wealth we see the virtuous Golden Dustman, golden in the metaphorical sense after all. And Bella's rejection of his values comes with the joy at knowing that Boffin is untarnished too.

She is always shown as partly affecting her mercenariness. Her declaration to her father, who asks her when she felt it 'coming on', has the tone of strained levity. When Boffin acts as devil's advocate his encouragement of her humour shows the gap between whole-hearted mercenariness and her half-hearted version:

49

'I hope, sir, you don't think me vain?' 'Not a bit, my dear,' said Mr Boffin. 'But I think it's very creditable in you, at your age, to be so well up with the pace of the world, and to know what to go in for. You are right. Go in for money, my love. Money's the article ...' (bk. III, ch. v)

The Brer Rabbit technique is of course powerful:

Somehow, Bella was not so well pleased with this assurance ... as she might have been. Somehow, when she put her arms round Mrs Boffin's neck and said Good-night, she derived a sense of unworthiness from the still anxious face of that good woman and her obvious wish to excuse her husband. 'Why, what need to excuse him?' thought Bella, sitting down in her own room. 'What he said was very sensible, I am sure, and very true, I am sure. It is only what I often say to myself. Don't I like it then? No, I don't like it, and, though he is my liberal benefactor, I disparage him for it.' (bk. III, ch. v)

Next Boffin enacts his full-blown miserly humour, and though it is studded with slight *double-entendres* which Dickens plainly enjoyed enormously ('Believe me that in spite of all the change in him, he is the best of men') the masquerade has all the plausible gusto of the impersonations of Edgar and Vendice. Mrs Boffin sheds real tears, for instance, though these are subsequently explained, but there are a number of details which perhaps explain why Gissing was convinced that Dickens had at one stage intended that Boffin should really turn miser. Bella is also in part acted on by genuine Good Angels, Lizzie Hexam and Harmon. Influenced from all sides she rejects Boffin after he explains to Harmon-Rokesmith, 'We all three know that it's Money she makes a stand for—money, money, money—and that you and your affections and hearts are a Lie, sir!' (bk. III, ch. xv). Then the deception thins gradually before the reader's eyes. Boffin snubs the Lammles and is shown on good terms with his wife.

When the final disclosure is made we are given two slightly different explanations. Boffin's version has the simple morality of a fairy-tale test:

> If she was to stand up for you when you was slighted, if she was to show herself of a generous mind when you was oppressed, if she was to be truest to you when you was poorest and friendliest, and all this against her own seeming interest, how would that do?' (bk. IV, ch. xiii)

This dovetails rather than conflicts with Bella's insight into the psychological machinery of her conversion:

> When you saw what a greedy little wretch you were the patron of, you determined to show her how much misused and misprized riches could do, and often had done, to spoil people; did you? Not caring what she thought of you (and Goodness knows *that* was of no consequence!) you showed her, in yourself, the most detestable sides of wealth, saying in your own mind, 'This shallow creature would never work the truth out of her own weak soul, if she had a hundred years to do it in; but a glaring instance kept before her may open even her eyes and set thinking.' (bk. IV, ch. xiii)

She calls Boffin her 'finger-post', just as Miss Havisham called Pip her looking-glass, and as Tattycoram saw in Miss Wade her own self grown ripe. This is the Dickensian version of the Whip and Bridle of Dante's Purgatory.

The moral stimulus of ideals and deterrents is not peculiar to Dickens's dramatization of change, but I know of no other novelist who uses this device with the consistency and emphasis which I have illustrated. In *Felix Holt*, for instance, to choose an example from a long novel, not a short fable like Poe's or Stevenson's, there are traces of this reliance on some concept of *similia similibus curantur*. Mrs Transome's portrait with its 'youthful brilliancy' contrasts with her present 'joyless, embittered age' to haunt Esther with a warning hint of her own possible future, rather as Darnay's face haunts Carton as a reminder of his possible past. But this warning mirror is only one item in a complex pattern of disenchantment, desire, and moral influence both implicit and explicit. George Eliot, like Jane Austen, presents human relationships as the most potent influence in conversion, and in their novels the didactic voice (Mr Knightley's or Daniel Deronda's) is stronger than any warning double. It might be argued that Dickens is summing up, in an especially condensed and theatrical way, these effects of human influence, but such argument obscures the suddenness of the vision— the 'glaring instance' works, or is made to appear to work, by empathy rather than instruction. And the diabolical enactment is usually more instructive than the ideal. Dickens's convention puts great responsibility on this single influence, and it is presented with the vividness of hallucination: Tattycoram and Bella see themselves in their potential doubles, and the act of seeing works the miracle.

It is not enough to dismiss the convention as an unrealistic, theatrical short-cut. It is a device which has to be related to the whole narrative context. This context is not exclusively concerned with moral analysis, and even though Dickens at times testifies to he gradualness of his conversions, he seems to need the economy of concentrated incident. In context, this is appropriate, and it is related to other features of the novels. The characters are not imaginatively analytical, and it would be futile to expect them to cope with the gradual piecemeal assembling of experience which is the central activity—the education in general truth—in many novels by George Eliot and James.[1] As Bella says, she needs 'the glaring instance'.

Condensation and theatrical vividness seem to be related to the passiveness of the converted characters. And this brings me to a brief comment on the gap between Dickens's moral action and his plot-action. In George Eliot and James the moral change determines the course of the action, though both novelists need to bring in the aids of accident and contrivance, and it is

[1] This kind of activity is usually missing in Dickens's portrayal of change. William James speaks of the sensation of detachment and passiveness which is a feature of many conversions: 'Throughout the height of it [the converting experience] he undoubtedly seems to himself a passive spectator or undergoer of an astounding process performed upon him from above.' Dickens's characters, unlike Defoe's and Dostoevsky's, do not have a feeling of sub-mission to an outside force, but rather give an impression of passive detach-ment. The conversion transforms a passive spectator rather than an active protagonist. One might pursue this passiveness and find resemblances to victims of brainwashing, or subjects of hypnosis and religious and political conversion. Like hypnosis or some forms of psycho-therapy, the Dickensian conversion involves an isolation of some aspect of personality for recognition. Like other forms of conversion, it may depend on change of environment, shock, fear, physiological lowering. And it works quickly. Dickens's own tendencies to hallucination and auto-suggestion, and his susceptibility to cyclical change, may account for some of these features. Humphry House's essay 'The Macabre Dickens' (which uses Edmund Wilson's essay on 'The Two Scrooges' and some comments by G. H. Lewes) includes suggestive remarks on the hallucinatory features of his treatment of villains which may apply also to the studies in conversion. But to argue in detail the psycho-logical validity of these conversions might both exaggerate and obscure their literary interest.

53

indeed an essential feature of George Eliot's action that chance or trivial action shall have great influence on destiny. But action is precipitated by the strengths and weaknesses of the characters, as when Maggie drifts away with Stephen, Dorothea marries Casaubon, or Daniel Deronda rescues Mirah. Martin Chuzzlewit, on the other hand, is a victim of Pecksniff rather than of his own egoism, Pip is trapped by Magwitch's gratitude, Bella's life is determined by a will and a benevolent intrigue. I do not want to exaggerate this passiveness: it is also true that Pip reacts to his great expectations as a proud and ungrateful boy, before they have worked on him strongly, and that Bella is susceptible to wealth's temptation. But the shape of the action is largely determined from outside. It has its origin in character, certainly: the plotting and mystery are not merely imposed by Dickens on his moral argument, but set going by Jonas Chuzzlewit, Dombey, Steerforth and Heep, Miss Havisham and Magwitch, Bradley Headstone, and John Jasper. It is, however, more often created by the villains than by the good or mixed characters. Even when it is created by a Magwitch, it is not Magwitch who is most changed by the action he precipitates. Gradgrind learns from the action he shapes and he and Dombey are perhaps closest to the typical hero of George Eliot and James in being changed by feeling the weight of their own action. But the vital difference between George Eliot's conversions and most of those in Dickens is that in George Eliot the character whose change is central to the action is changed in and by the action he initiates, in the process of recognizing moral causality and responsibility. Dickens's

54

characters, further removed from this kind of tragic process, are changed less by seeing what they have done than by seeing what they are, and in the exaggerated form of 'the glaring instance'. Dickens's segregated and sensational converting vision is appropriate to, and perhaps to some extent produced by, his concept of action.

He is too interested in social satire, comic incident, and melodramatic intrigue and mystery, to give more space to moral action. This comment is not intended to ignore his simplified and sometimes cursory treatment of character, but even where the psychology is blunt—and it is not always—this is only a negative explanation of his treatment of moral change. It is as if he were committed to the imposed external action of some eighteenth-century novels, like those of Fielding and Smollett, which he had read and admired. Wilkie Collins may have followed him, or added his influence in this kind of plotting. But the interest of moral change in Collins is small, for his concept of character is much more arbitrary and plot-determined than Dickens's. Dickens's division into plotters and victims, and his frequent separation of moral change and adventure, bring him closer to Fielding and Smollett—in spite of the contemporary relevance of his *roman policier*—than to his fellow-Victorians. But he uses this split action and imposed plot for the expression of an essentially nineteenth-century theme, that theme of the growth of love and social sense which may be more subtly explored by greater psychologists than Dickens, but which still shapes his moral categories. Even if his psychology is stereotyped, his categories melodramatically distinct, part of the force of his conversions lies in

55

the implication that the mixed character, the redeemable Tattycoram or Bella, has an affinity with the riper and purer evil. It is this threat of affinity which makes the fingerpost an effective warning. The moral trap set by Harmon and Boffin for Bella is very like the trap set for Pecksniff by old Martin's impersonation: but Pecksniff is confirmed in his humour, not converted. Where Dickens appears to be using a fantastic machinery akin to the techniques of eighteenth-century fiction, he can come close to the moral truth aimed at by his contemporaries. The enactment of conversion, the very hinge of the true novel of moral development, is more than an interesting and consistent technical device for it seems to reveal some of the ways in which Dickens's imagination does and does not work.

3 The Change of Heart (2)

Underlying the conversions in most of Dickens's novels, then, is this fallacy that correlates vision and action. The converted heroes undergo a change of heart by looking within, seeing the fault, and changing their lives, and Dickens does not show us this process in a slow minute analysis but outlines it simply and broadly, summarizing and dramatizing his psychological insight. A more acute insight into the division between vision and action, is embodied in four of his most interesting women characters, Edith Dombey, Louisa Bounderby, Estella, and Bella Wilfer. Once more, an insight into human morality and action is outlined rather than detailed, but this time the pattern is more complex. My excuse for writing an unfashionable character study is threefold: this group of characters reveals an interesting insight, the ways of dramatizing that insight, and—to my mind—a certain degeneration and decline. Readers interested in questions of biography will notice that the novels I am concerned with cover twenty years, from 1846 (*Dombey and Son*) to 1865 (*Our Mutual Friend*) and that two of them precede, while two succeed, Dickens's acquaintance with Ellen Ternan.

Martin Chuzzlewit, Scrooge, and David Copperfield embody the straightforward movement from seeing to doing, and may well leave us with the impression that they are unimaginative characters who need the clarification and stimulus of external models. They first see themselves in the true or distorting mirrors outside themselves. Edith, Louisa, Estella, and Bella are, on the contrary, given more imagination than they can comfortably contain. Their long and tortuous conflicts and conversions take place as inner action, within the mind, on the stage of private reflection and feeling. The converted heroes are analysed and dramatized in external action, like figures in a Morality Play, neither self-contained nor unified, but the converted heroines are analysed and dramatized as realistic characters involved in a complex process. It is a process most coherently shown in Edith, then imitated and revised, with varying degrees of incoherence and ellipsis, in her successors.

Dickens is a novelist who constantly struggles to show inner action in the theatre of the outer action in which his imagination was most vitally and easily at home. The four women characters I am discussing are attempts at inner action, and are at the same time exposures of a perverting social environment. As women, unfitted by education to move against the environment, they are malleable, victimized, and vividly able to show the distorting source. Each of them is passive, up to a point, and each is at the same time hostile to the very social forces to which she submits.

Edith, Louisa, Estella, and Bella are schooled by an acquisitive society for a certain kind of marriage, and for a certain kind of culture. Mrs Skewton, Gradgrind, Miss Havisham, and Mrs Wilfer, are the parents who represent various sexual, cultural, political, and educational pressures. They are themselves most expressive social symbols, Mrs Skewton and Mrs Wilfer violently grotesque extremes, Miss Havisham and Gradgrind themselves cases of conversion. Dickens is interested in these bad fathers and mothers, and also interested in the larger societies and institutions that they represent. The daughters show the corruption of love, marriage, and maternity. George Eliot and Henry James see women as the 'frail vessels' who carry the treasure of human feeling through the generations, and most of their vessels are very weak or very strong. Dickens may be a much cruder psychologist than his great successors but he is closer to psychic and social realities in his treatment of the hardened and perverted vessel.

The four heroines see themselves for what they are, and dislike what they see. Bella is the only one whose insight is given an external prompting (by the disguised Boffin), and this makes her declare her feelings, rather than actually change them. They are all given the imaginative and rational capacity for this moral insight and judgment, but they are also given marketable qualities of charm and beauty, and a strong susceptibility to the market values. They have something of the off-hand and careless elegance, *ennui*, and recklessness of the dandies, Steerforth, Wrayburn, and Harthouse, qualities which combine to make a mocking mask for their ambivalence. In their sensuality and their exposure to experience they are as different as they could be from the complacencies of Dickens's ideals, Agnes or Esther Summerson, and have most in common with the prostitute with the heart of gold, Nancy or Martha,

59

as Edith clearly sees, drawing her mother's attention to it in a fine ironic flight.

Edith Dombey is the finest and fullest analysis of the type. She is not usually looked on as a psychologically complex character. H. W. Garrod dismisses her as 'improbable', Kathleen Tillotson reads her character acutely but says much more about the theatricality of her presentation, and A. O. Cockshut gives her a good deal of thought, ultimately concludes that she is unsuccessful, and indeed questions that very element of 'self-immolation' which interests Kathleen Tillotson. He finds it hard to believe in Edith's insight:

> Edith sees the similarity [between herself and Alice Marwood] even before her marriage, which would require exceptional qualities of detachment and self-analysis. And Dickens is unable to persuade us that Edith possesses them. He is guilty here of a failing very common in novelists of strong convictions—he is making a character do the author's work for him by commenting (as if from above) upon her own personality. (*The Imagination of Charles Dickens* (London, 1961), p. 105.)

Cockshut is seizing on a genuine weakness of Dickens's art—it is quite true that he is a novelist who presses his characters promiscuously into the service of explicitness. But the weakness of the parallelism observed by Edith is surely its tautology, rather than its unconvincing psychology. I see Edith as a character whose detachment, self-analysis, and insight are important, conscious, and fundamental and, far from being implausible, most coherent and sustained. She shows Dickens's interest in characters with sensitive moral insight whose actions go against the grain of their

60

insight. Where he and other Victorian novelists are unrealistic and unpersuasive, it is not in characters like this, for all their theatricality of portraiture, but in the cases where insight and action go neatly hand-in-hand along the straight and narrow road. Edith and her descendants see the better but follow the worse. Out of a complex moral experience comes a constant play of irony in their attitudes both to their superior insight and their inferior actions. So many of Dickens's moral touchstones are achieved by crude simplification that we should appreciate even the inflation of Edith's Mephistophelean despair, with its pride, *ennui*, irony, and ambiguous cruelty.

When we first see her, through Dombey's eyes in Chapter xxi, the chief impression is of world-weariness. Dickens uses a rather fidgety and inappropriate gestural method to convey this: of course Edith would not have gone in for all this tossing and drooping:

Walking by the side of the chair, and carrying her gossamer parasol with a proud and weary air, as if so great an effort must be soon abandoned and the parasol dropped, sauntered a much younger lady, very handsome, very haughty, very wilful, who tossed her head and dropped her eyelids, as though, if there were anything in all the world worth looking into, save a mirror, it certainly was not the earth or sky.

Edith's *blasé* sophistication is a social and a moral attitude, an elegant affectation and a social contempt actually earned by familiarity with affectation. Her refusal to be enthusiastic, for instance, is both a fashionable gesture and a criticism of her mother's false enthusiasms. The weariness is also something deeper. It is a very real fatigue caused by the hard work

61

of constant unnatural performance and advertisement. This moral disgust and exhaustion belonged to Dickens's original conception of her character, 'Proud and weary of her degradation'. The critical and self-critical implications of what might seem merely elegant display are picked up sharply, from the beginning, by her persistent criticism of her mother. The mask of world-weariness may hide almost any kind of insecurity or false security, but in Edith it is a mask for moral energy. The self-contemptuous heroines have plenty of contempt for the unequivocally defective characters around them. Edith directs her contempt against her mother, Major Bagstock, Dombey, and Carker. She exposes and undercuts her mother's enthusiasms and affectations, faintly, loudly, coldly, almost humorously. Kathleen Tillotson is right in denying her that 'flash of wit' which might make her an Edith Newcome (though I think Thackeray's Edith is a much more simple character), but there is one occasion when she is given a flicker of dark humour—'the twilight of a smile'—as she comments on her mother's rejection of their possible associates, 'They have not enough heart'.

She is presented from the outset, not as a proud and mercenary character, strangely aware of her own defects, but as a proud and honest character naturally aware of her defects. Her sophistication works on a superficial level, on which she traps Dombey; and on a profound level, on which she attempts to transform herself and Dombey. The odd thing about Edith is not her moral awareness but her immoral actions. Her mercenary heartlessness, for instance, is demonstrated in her actions, in her two marriages, but nowhere in her reasoning or quality of feeling. But there is no mistake about her two marriages. She commits herself to the values she criticizes. If it is her insight which strikes us as unlikely, that must be a result of remembering rather than reading the character. Our very first impression is that of a sensitive *ennui*, a wide-awake weariness, an appropriate cynicism, appearing as it does in the context of Mrs Skewton's false vitality and Dombey's self-absorbed reserve and cold boredom. If we look closely at the interactions of character we can see a dense and intricate structure of relationship which makes character vivid and values sharp.

Edith's refusal to be enthusiastic during her courtship by Dombey brings out the ambivalence of her *ennui*. Her bored acquiescence in his wishes is bound up with her refusal to show enthusiasm for art and nature, insincerely admired by the other characters. What is honest in her unenthusiastic reaction to nature is also honest in her unenthusiastic reaction to Dombey. Neutral is not quite the word for this lack of enthusiasm, since Dickens shows us some conflict. She displays her accomplishments with no show of feeling, and no appearance of pleasing. She answers Dombey's questions monosyllabically, 'with a strange reluctance; and with that remarkable air of opposition to herself, already noticed as belonging to her beauty. Yet she was not embarrassed, but wholly self-possessed.' The movement from self-criticism is smooth: what she opposes in herself is her identification with the Skewton/ Bagstock market values. When she is left alone with her mother and Major Bagstock she drops all reserve in a blunt and ironical contempt which snubs pretences: 'It is surely not worth while, Mama ... to observe these forms of speech. We are quite alone. We know each other'; and 'Not woman yet?' and 'Will I go!' Dickens adds the gloss, 'The quiet scorn that sat upon her handsome face—a scorn that evidently lighted on herself, no less than them—was so intense and deep, that her mother's simper, for the instant, though of a hardy constitution, drooped before it.'

The genuine *ennui* often functions as a mask. There is one scene where Edith is discovered alone by Carker, and which shows the same reliance on visual signs and gestures that we saw in the introductory tossing and drooping. Dickens's scenic imagination can produce the fine effects of the Artful Dodger swinging his leg while Oliver timidly and gratefully cleans his boots, or of Bradley Headstone beating his hand on the stone, but he can also over-produce his characters, and present them as if they were actors instead of characters in fiction. It is not simply that he is being unnecessarily explicit but rather that certain characters would not put on this kind of performance. But the plot is served by the mopping and mowing, because Carker has to be able to spy out Edith's inner conflict. What is equally convenient fine perceptiveness in a novel by Henry James, comes out as a crude sign-language in Dickens. Carker cannot fail to read the grimaces and gesticulations which are rendered almost nonsensical by Dickens's insistence on Edith's control and reserve. Nonsense hovers perilously near the phrase 'almost the self-same glance':

It was that of a lady, elegantly dressed and very handsome, whose dark proud eyes were fixed upon the ground, and in whom some passion or struggle was raging. For as she sat looking down, she held a corner of her under lip within her mouth, her bosom heaved, her nostril quivered, her head trembled, indignant tears were on her cheek, and her foot was set upon the moss as though she would have crushed it into nothing. And yet almost the self-same glance that showed him this, showed him the self-same lady rising with a scornful air of weariness and lassitude, and turning away with nothing expressed in face or figure but care-less beauty and imperious disdain. (ch. xxvii)

Everything about this scene is over-contrived—situation, language, gesture, movement. Dickens can use sign-language without such strain or grossness, as in Chapter xl, where Dombey interviews Edith in her room: all the visual detail is pressed into strong symbolic significance—her appearance, the room itself, dress, jewels, objects. There is the single ludicrous touch of the movement of her diamond necklace—a marriage gift—which 'rose and fell impatiently upon her bosom, seemed to pant to break the chain that clasped them round her neck, and roll down on the floor where she might tread them'. This Ouida-like animation antici-pates the moment when she takes off her jewels and stamps on them, but it is the only detail in the scene which is false and uncontrolled. Otherwise, everything works delicately, both as surface and symbol. Dombey is very naturally embarrassed and awkward as he stands amongst the splendid feminine disarray, reading its signs of contempt, rejection, wealth, and voluptuous-ness. Dickens emphasizes Edith's physical beauty and 'cold composure' in what is a scene of some sexual significance, marking Dombey's invasion of intimacy and Edith's resistance. The very disarray of the room is

65

private and repulsive, and felt as both by Dombey who
has by now learnt to read Edith's carelessness more
accurately:

He felt this disadvantage, and he showed it. Solemn and
strange among this wealth of colour and voluptuous glitter,
strange and constrained towards its haughty mistress, whose
repellent beauty it repeated, and presented all around him, as in
so many fragments of a mirror, he was conscious of embarrass-
ment and awkwardness. Nothing that ministered to her disdain-
ful self-possession could fail to gall him.

The scene marks a crisis in Dombey's understanding of
Edith. Her passivity, acquiescence, coldness, and lack
of show once lured, flattered, and suited him. Neither
compliment nor compatibility last very long, and
Dombey comes to find the answer to the question
Dickens asked earlier:

Whether she held cheap, attractions that could only call forth
admiration that was worthless to her, or whether she designed to
render them more precious to admirers by this usage of them,
those to whom they *were* precious seldom paused to consider.

By the time he comes to deliver his ultimatum in the
boudoir scene, Dombey sees that her negligence was
rebellion, her coldness contempt, her haughtiness not
an accessory to his but separate and opposed. Up to this
point there is perhaps some ambiguity for the reader too:
behind that mask Edith cannot be entirely unaware of
its charm, but despite the ambiguity, she has in a sense
played fair, worn her heartlessness on her sleeve,
reduced the courtship to its bare structure of buying
and selling. Her response is misread by Dombey, but
nevertheless says, 'I have no feeling for you, and will

66

pretend to none.' One of the weaknesses in the latter treatment of the Dombey marriage is her social beha-viour. The refusal to entertain Dombey's guests is not very plausible or even consistent, though it extends her contemptuous and critical attitude to the false and mercenary environment. What we really need here is more intimate detail of Dombey's expectations of submission and her refusal, but the stress that is laid on her conduct as a hostess is not quite in keeping with the cool but decorous performance she puts on willingly enough—if carelessly—when she shows her paces with the brush and on the harp. What does emerge, despite the reticence and external treatment, is the trapped innocence of both Edith and Dombey: if she plays fair according to her code, it is in just the way which he is bound to misinterpret. Her fair dealing is invisible to his huge vanity.

Edith is a character whose complexity defines the moral values of the novel both negatively and positively, and she stands out as a much more interesting and particularized human case than the simple good characters like Paul, Florence, Toots, Cap'n Cuttle, and Sol, who all criticize worldliness from a kind of holy and protected innocence. A. O. Cockshut remarks that Dickens's good characters make goodness seem very easy. Characters like Edith are important because they make goodness seem very hard. She finds falsity and greed rewarded, honesty and feeling punished by humiliation and weariness, and in this context she achieves a form of earned cynicism. The process shows the sheer difficulty of change, solicited as she is by the ease of habit, and by a reluctant pride. Dickens shows

F   67 her ultimately retreating in pride, exhaustion, and self-doubt from the possibility of conversion, and choosing a perverse revenge on Dombey, Carker, and herself.

The flight with Carker is the climax of her pride, honesty, and self-contempt. The adultery which Dickens first intended and the substituted rejection of Carker both fit the psychological pattern. In rejecting her seducer she uses him, humiliatingly, as a mask, giving him the name of seducer in order to ruin Dombey and herself, but in the process executing a spirited and subtle sexual revenge on the man who has seen through her reserve. Her recklessness in marrying Dombey is outdone and undone by the greater recklessness of leaving him. The development in perverse moral action comes most logically after she has received her purchase money and after she meets Florence, when she feels her heart touched but feels too—especially when her offer to attempt a decent life is dismissed by Dombey—that salvation is too difficult. In the circumstances, damnation seems the only honest course. Dickens calls her 'a woman with a noble quality yet dwelling in her nature, who was too false to her better self, and too debased and lost, to save herself'. The moral action is more subtle than this summary suggests. It is another case of having to trust the tale, not the artist. The complexity of her moral perversion is more fairly imaged in one of the stagey gestures, when on the eve of her marriage she 'cruelly grasped her bosom with her hand' and averted her head, 'as if she would avoid the sight of her own fair person, and divorce herself from its companionship'. In a later image Dickens shows her not averting her head, but looking at Carker and

68

holding it up 'as if she were a beautiful Medusa, looking at him, face to face, to strike him dead'. She is a Medusa destroyed by her own image.

It is tempting to think of her self-contempt and perversion as springing from her appreciation of absolutes. Dickens was neither Byron nor Baudelaire, and the Satanism of Edith is blurred and incomplete, something only approaching the fallen angel's feeling for the lost light. But it is worth noticing that such a comparison at least arises, even if it is dismissed as inappropriate.

Dickens was so interested in this moral pattern, that he returned to it on several occasions, though with steadily decreasing control and completeness after *Dombey and Son*. We tend to see development and progression in the art of Dickens but this group of characters is a case of the degeneration of a formula. Edith belonged to the Dombey world, and attempts to transplant her to other worlds were not wholly successful. When we move to Louisa in *Hard Times* the same mould is being used, but less clearly and certainly. *Hard Times* is a novel more narrowly concerned with education than *Dombey and Son*, where it had been one of several subjects. In place of Mrs Skewton's unprincipled and grasping stupidity we have the high-principled rationality of Gradgrind. Mrs Skewton affects feeling but knows nothing whatsoever about it. Gradgrind affects a rational repudiation of feeling, but in nearly everything he actually does during the novel itself he comes out as rather amiable and even affectionate. Like Edith, Louisa is educated perversely, trained to repress and deny warmth and impulse, and

69

like Edith, she makes a loveless marriage, breaks with it violently, almost but not quite committing adultery, repents and is forgiven. Like Edith, though much earlier in her life, Louisa is touched by a revealing affection, for her brother Tom.

We may see Gradgrind's amiability in realization and coldness in theory as the result of a realistic typology, where the character contains but is not contained by its humour. But we may also object that he is such a nice man that his daughter's marriage is grossly unmotivated. Gradgrind does not drive her, as Mrs Skewton drives Edith, but merely puts Bounderby's proposal before her 'on grounds of reason and calculation'. He reveals no very mercenary calculating motive and even asks Louisa, rather uneasily, if she has any other attachment. He stands back while she makes her decision, only making the point that love is a meaningless concept and that individual disparity of age is statistically insignificant. When he takes in Sissy, and when he speaks to his children, even before the change of heart, there is nothing monstrous about him except the actual theorizing that comes out of his mouth. This makes, I think, for a certain shadowiness in the environment and motives of Louisa. *Hard Times*, for a long time the only Dickens novel approved by F. R. Leavis, shows a certain lack of concreteness if we put it beside *Dombey and Son*.

Louisa, again like Edith, speaks in ironies and ambiguities which are read in one way by the characters and another by the reader. She too makes no claims when Bounderby woos her, and her honesty gives her the appearance of an inviting cool rationality which attracts him and suits him. Much of her irony is literally true, and its impact lies in the reception it gets from her husband and her father who can see nothing wrong in it: 'You have been so careful of me, that I never had a child's heart. You have trained me so well, that I never dreamed a child's dream.' Her reserve hides the complaint and the appeal: only the wise can hear the indictment. It is Gradgrind's rational inability to speak and understand that so nearly ruins his daughter. But as there is a gap between Gradgrind's saying and doing, so Louisa herself is not quite a coherent character. She asks him certain questions in order to test him, but she also seems passively and exhaustedly rational, in part conditioned by her nurture, in part rejecting it. This is a less well-knit study of self-immolation than the analysis of Edith. Louisa's marriage with Bounderby actually takes place less because of Gradgrind's influence than because of Tom, whom Louisa loves and thinks she can help through the marriage. It is heart, and irrationality, rather than a cold appraisal and calculation, which make the marriage. Dickens seems to be writing locally rather than from a full sense of his own narrative when at the end he makes Louisa blame her father without saying a word about the influence of her feeling for her brother. In fact, when we pursue this psychological questioning, the characters in this novel will not stand up to it, but reveal themselves as shifting in form and content from place to place, rather like characters in a Jacobean tragedy, where we may be required to pity in one scene what we condemn in the next, without fitting together the separate emotional and psychological stimulae into a single and unified 'character'. Edith stands up to this kind of questioning, not Louisa.

Louisa is sufficiently of one piece to move us and interest us: it is only this kind of psychological scrutiny which disintegrates a character quite strong enough for local appeal. She speaks both sensitively and meaninglessly—for Gradgrind—when she uses a metaphorical language which the literal-minded cannot possibly read, pointing to the Coketown chimneys, where there seems 'to be nothing but languid and monotonous smoke. But when the night comes, Fire bursts out. ...' She is plausibly shown as shrinking from Sissy's insight and pity, in a mixture of resentment and pride, and in her constraint and carelessness with Harthouse. The reaction to Sissy is a little like Edith's reaction to Florence, and Harthouse is of course a new version of the rejected seducer, though he is treated more seriously and let off more lightly than Carker. Louisa's marriage is shown in anti-feminine detail which functions like the imagery of Edith's rich and splendid boudoir: there is carelessness and contempt here too:[1]

She was so constrained, and yet so careless; so reserved, and yet so watchful; so cold and proud, and yet so sensitively ashamed of her husband's braggart humility ... Utterly indifferent, perfectly self-reliant, never at a loss, and yet never at her ease ...

No graceful little adornment, no fanciful little device, however trivial, anywhere expressed her influence. Cheerless and comfortless, boastfully and doggedly rich, there the room stared at its present occupants, unsoftened and unrelieved by the least trace of any womanly occupation. (bk. ii, ch. ii)

[1] The conscious cultivation of the image of the tomboy—in Maggie Tulliver, Louisa Alcott's Jo, and many others, is plainly a social symbol (in life and literature) of considerable interest to the historian of feminism.

Dickens is of course not simply repeating himself. Harthouse, for instance, offers Louisa the persuasion of a nihilism for which her mind is already prepared, in reasoning and in despair. But she shows the duality of Edith: 'struggling disposition to believe in a wider and nobler humanity' and—as she sees herself imaged in Tom—'mistaken ... misconceived ... misdirected'. This conflict is given a strong and lively personality: just as Edith's chief characteristic was a sophisticated world-weariness, so Louisa's is a rather *farouche* reserve. Beneath the surface, Edith was a case of coherent and complex psychological analysis; beneath the surface, Louisa is made up of more discrete though locally effective details that do not quite fit together. Louisa, and her relationships, come from a more cursory exploration of moral causality, and the comparison with *Dombey and Son* brings this home.

Estella, in *Great Expectations*, is also cast in this rather worn mould. Once more Dickens is showing a divided character, though this is to be inferred, not straightforwardly and clearly read. In Edith's case we are very emphatically told that she is divided, and the division is fully analysed and animated. In Louisa's case we are told so again, though the actual dramatization does not make it very plain, and the perversity of her actions is rather sketchily explained. In Estella's case, Dickens seems uncertain about the relation of appearance and inner life: A. O. Cockshut describes her as 'lamenting the absence of feelings she has never had', but lamenting does not seem quite the word for her detached account. The difficulty in *Hard Times* is in accepting Louisa's actions, which seem unrelated to her visible moral insight. The difficulty in *Great Expectations* is in accepting the combination of coldness and insight in an opaque character whom we never see through. We are not told of the tensions of pride, reserve, and self-immolation beneath the cold surface but Dickens leaves it for us to read between the lines, with the aid perhaps of a few hints, such as her refusal to marry Pip because she does not want to hurt him, and her decision to marry Bartley Drummle, from a mixture of spite and masochism, because his is a heart she seems to want to break: in these twin negative and positive decisions there is a moral value and feeling. She is a strong critic of the values of the environment, as in her speech about Miss Havisham's legacy-hunters:

> You had not your little wits sharpened by their intrigue against you, suppressed and defenceless, under the mask of sympathy and pity and what not, that is soft and soothing.—I had. You did not gradually open your round childish eyes wider and wider to the discovery of that imposter of a woman who calculates her stores of peace of mind for when she wakes up in the night. (ch. xxxiii)

Estella's account of her own heartlessness, and her refusal to feel anything for Miss Havisham, is to a large extent undercut by her criticisms of the really heartless characters. Not only is she not revealed from the inside, but she is not given the touches of strong feeling, like Edith's for Florence and Louisa's for Tom. Moreover, she is shown as a much harder and nastier character than either Edith or Louisa, in her contempt for Pip, at least in their younger days. But she is shown as apparently softening: she is honest with Pip and warns him, she shrinks from the sight of Jaggers's house. And her final offstage conversion is only explicable if we read reserve, pride, and self-contempt into her apparently single-minded actions. She is a puzzling character, best explained as another looser and vaguer version of Edith.

The enabling act of moral insight which is fully dramatized in Edith, more incoherent in Louisa, and only implied in Estella, is last seen in Bella Wilfer. She too attacks the bad parent and is at last converted, to public choice rather than to a fundamental change of heart, by the moral impersonations of Harmon Rokesmith and Boffin. Bella is a vaguer and much softer version of Edith Dombey's moral character. Rather like George Eliot's Esther in *Felix Holt* she has her moral problem made easy by the combined solicitations of love and duty. Bella is a much less clear-sighted and intelligent character than the other three, needing her 'glaring instance', as she calls it. There is on first sight her petulance and impatience, shown promisingly directed against the empty, affected and cruel talk of that great comic character, Mrs Wilfer. There is her affection for her father. And there is her resentment of being treated as property and willed as a legacy. Later we see less self-contempt than contempt for Rokesmith, quickly followed by repentance. On the same page as her thought that he is 'keeping eligible people off' is her quick response to his hint that she is neglecting her family. She makes the long speech to her father about being mercenary and looking out for money to captivate, but the whole interview is so teasing, generous and punctuated by her embarrassingly affectionate hair-dressing that we have to endorse his feeble 'It would be

75

quite so, if you fully knew what you said, my dear, or meant it' when she asks, 'Isn't it shocking?' The playful tone and lack of any moral action is far removed from the perversions of Edith. At the end of Chapter iv she talks about 'Money, money, money', but all she actually does is to shrink from Boffin's miserly humour. The Boffin plot turns out to be more a testing and revealing of Bella's worth for Harmon's benefit, as it was originally conceived, than the moral stimulus it is eventually said to be. The temptation by Another, in this case Lightwood, is so very lightly sketched in as to be significantly forgettable. There is no active endorsement for her own comment: 'I am convinced I have no heart as people call it; and I think that sort of thing is nonsense.' When she is with Lizzie, to whom she responds with significant admiration and tenderness, we see that Dickens is perhaps deliberately lightening her weight: 'The wayward, playful, affectionate nature, giddy for want of the weight of some sustaining purpose, and capricious because it was always fluttering among little things. ...' When at the end she says, 'I have been so much worse', we cannot feel that this has been shown in action. 'Worldly, shallow, sordid, vain': all the words used of her, except 'shallow', fit Estella and Edith, but not Bella. All she has actually *done* is to refuse Rokesmith (once) unfairly and rudely, and even then she manages to get in a word about not being as bad as he probably thinks she is. Her pride has little social significance but looks more like a shy and ambivalent sexual pride. I find it very strange that Angus Wilson should call her 'the most developed heroine in Dickens's fiction' ('The Heroes and

76

Heroines of Dickens', *A Review of English Literature*, ii, 3, July 1961), and even stranger that Edgar Johnson feels not only her power but her fatality:

> Bella's venality is not just one girl's greed, it is the dominant and cherished vice of pecuniary society and Bella ... is seen with a deeper and more intimate and less dazzled understanding even than Pip's disillusioned knowledge of the fatal and tormenting creature who rung his heart. In her selfishness and charm and greed for money and playful tenderness, she is drawn with a wonderful and compelling clarity that imposes an absolute conviction of her irresistible fascination. Nor does one doubt the sweep of indignant emotion with which she repudiates her own mercenary greed, although one may feel a little less assured of that conversion to unselfish devotion. (*Charles Dickens* (London, 1953), Part ix, Chapter v)

I find it easier to accept the conversion than the mercenary greed, as I have tried to show, but the word I want to repudiate is Johnson's 'clarity'. Edith's complex moral composition and process was clear, Louisa's, Estella's, and Bella's much less so. It is tempting to describe Dickens's characters, and not to analyse them, but only a fairly prolonged analysis can consider the relation between character and action, a relation which is often unsteady and superficial. The group of characters I have discussed seems to show that such unsteadiness and insufficiency may have been the result of his reluctance to discard an old mould. What begins as a brilliant insight and coherent realization in *Dombey and Son* first becomes mechanized then disintegrates.

77

Particular

4 *Pickwick Papers*

Some recent critics have tended to see *Pickwick Papers* as a fable, and I think it is probably true that it is more like a fable than any of Dickens's other long works of fiction, though a purer example of Dickensian fable is *A Christmas Carol. Pickwick Papers* makes no use of fantasy in its main action but up to a point it can be read as a fable. It proffers pastoral and domestic symbols of the good life, its events and characters present moral concepts by side-stepping social and psychological complication. Like fable, it has a simply extractable point, and like fable it makes no attempt to show the difficulties and subtleties of leading the good life or passing ethical judgments, but tends to suggest that conduct and moral judgment are clear and simple processes. It is like a fable in some ways, but in others not at all.

If we read or re-read its 800 odd pages after being stimulated by the interpretations of Dostoevsky, or W. H. Auden, or Steven Marcus, it may well be that we emerge wishing, with some feelings of disappointment, that it were more like a Christian fable than it really is. To say it is a fable is to pick on certain features and ignore others, and some of the ignored features are really rather weak and tedious. It is much easier to see the structure and statement of *Pickwick Papers* at a considerable distance from the full text itself, and I want to argue that if we are to understand and judge its individual qualities as a work of art, and if we are to see its place in Dickens's work, we should keep close to its detail, and try to say something about its variety. We must lay less stress on its resemblance to the Don Quixote story (Dostoevsky) its mythical rendering of the Fall from innocence to a knowledge of the world (Auden) or its revelations of the transcendent possibilities of human goodness (Marcus) and try to say something about the bits that do not fit into such mythical patterns.

I would not suggest that there is nothing in any of these interpretations. There are many points at which they fit *Pickwick Papers* extraordinarily well, considering the number of points where the fit is either very loose or rather a squeeze. I do think they tell us rather more about the mythopoeic powers of modern criticism than about the actual workings of Dickens's mythopoeic imagination, but it is not my purpose here to take issue on the many ways of extracting and abstracting ideas from works of art—such extraction is an interesting and legitimate activity if we see what it is that we are doing. *Pickwick Papers* is a very large and rambling novel, a real loose baggy monster, and I have often found that in attempting to give some account of its many features, I have succeeded in forgetting and neglecting much that seems striking when actually reading the book. All I want to say here is that *Pickwick Papers* is a novel from which symbols and interpretations can be very easily extracted while leaving the critic with interesting materials still on his hands. Of

82

course we can see a moral, and Pickwick tells us what it is, though heroes are not always the most reliable guides. This is how Pickwick sums up his career, in a conclusion which sounds more modest than it really is:

I shall never regret having devoted the greater part of two years to mixing with different varieties and shades of human character: frivolous as my pursuit of novelty may have appeared to many. Nearly the whole of my previous life having been devoted to business and the pursuit of wealth, numerous scenes of which I had no previous conception have dawned upon me—I hope to the enlargement of my mind, and the improvement of my understanding. If I have done but little good, I trust I have done less harm, and that none of my adventures will be other than a source of amusing and pleasant recollection to me in the decline of life. God bless you all!

Pickwick himself is a peg on which possibilities are slung rather than a character capable of demonstrating anything like the change implied here: not only are we shown neither the early stage of business nor the pursuit of wealth, but Pickwick's large sweet innocence is utterly incompatible with any such experience. It is true that he sees certain facts and sees through certain illusions, but Dickens makes no attempt to demonstrate enlargement of mind or improvement of understanding: the words are the grandiose words of a conclusion, and, if anyone doubts this, the fairest comparison could be made within Dickens's work, with the conversion of Scrooge. (Comparisons with Don Quixote or Adam or Christ are less useful.)

The study of imperfect works of art is an interesting and far from useless activity, but I must make it plain that I am less concerned to mark down *Pickwick Papers* than to try to get close to it. Reading, as opposed to reading into, those 800 pages is a very bumpy and fragmented experience. We move through dazzlingly funny stretches and some poignant moments, through passages of tedium which do indeed tend to vanish from the memory once we are actually away from the reading experience. Dickens is at his least gripping in the passages of description in *Pickwick Papers*, and there are many rural scenes and domestic interiors (easily forgotten, and indeed easily skipped) which show nothing of his ability to animate a scene by keeping his eye on the nature of objects or by a grotesque metaphorical projection. Nor is he very successful in horseplay, which is all too dominant, especially in the early chapters. The celebrated macabre stories have a few fine moments of passion and sensation, but much crude, strained, and stereotyped writing. The novel is also most interestingly lacking in self-consciousness, and can invoke our pity for starvation on one page while demanding our delight in high living on the next. This kind of disintegration Dickens took a long time to grow out of. The *power* of *Pickwick Papers* could not be less like the *power* of a fable, for it resides in parts rather than in the whole, and in parts not very strongly attached to each other in feeling or moral argument. Its power lies primarily in its comedy, but by no means in all its comic scenes or in all its comic characters. Dickens is weak in rendering his comedy of humours, and is weak in farce. But he is very strong in comic wit, joke, and anecdote, and perhaps most successful in his mixture of the comic and the macabre. Dickens's comedy needs the stiffening either of satire or of the macabre, and where his comedy is neither satiric nor dark it is always least successful. Few of the inset tales that are entirely serious escape crudity of language and feeling, though they have the advantage over the purely comic scenes of farce in having some tension and point. The strength of *Pickwick Papers* lies in grotesque or satiric comedy that is toughened, blackened, and enlarged in context; its weakness lies in horseplay and comic character that is muted, mild, and cut-off from the realities it pretends to mock. In some ways he outgrew *Pickwick Papers*, in some ways its limits remained his limits. And in some ways its archness and mildness in comedy is the archness and mildness not only of Dickens, but of other instances of Victorian sensibility.

First let me say something about the book's obvious weaknesses. The usual placing of *Pickwick Papers* in the Dickens canon goes something like this: it shows an advance, in comedy and in organization, on the frankly discrete episodes which make up *Sketches by Boz*, and it picks up in tautness and focus as it develops from the original script for Seymour's sporting-life illustrations into something like a novel's tension and unity of action. The tension and unity are analysed roughly like this: the early disconnected episodes are gradually brought into some order and concentration with the case of *Bardell* v. *Pickwick*, which lands Pickwick in the Fleet, from which point the novel becomes darker, sterner, more profound, and more realistic. All recent accounts of the novel also pay proper attention to the way in which the comic surface of the action is deeply furrowed by the macabre and violent inset stories of madness, suffering, poverty, and crime.

85

All this is quite true. The defect of it as formal analysis (and as anything else) is that it is highly selective and very incomplete. *Sketches by Boz*, for all its lack of continuity, is to my mind more morally and sociologically unified than *Pickwick Papers*, more freely and more totally satiric and compassionate. The relation of *Pickwick Papers* to later Dickensian successes is rather weakly explained if we concentrate our attention on slackness as contrasted with tightness, on episodic as contrasted with centripetal form. It seems more important to point out that as the novel developed Dickens came to acquire not so much a sense of form as a sense of comedy. Sales picked up tremendously when Sam Weller came in, not, I think, because his entry was the beginning of a unified plot and a coherent moral development but because he brought originality and definition into some very floppy horseplay and some rather uncertain comedy of character. Jingle had helped, in the wild flights of language and fantasy which outdo and outwit the feeble aspirations and innocence of the Pickwick Club, but Sam Weller brought comedy into goodness itself. He also propped up the humours of Pickwick and his friends, acting as a kind of comic bridge between the comic rogues (Jingle and Trotter) and the comic fools (the Pickwickians). The comic scenes become balanced and sharp. Jingle and Trotter begin a Jonsonian tug-of-war with Weller, matched as they are in wit and cunning. And Dickens finds something to do with horseplay: he makes it satirical, in the political scenes of Eatanswill, the social scenes of Bath, and the religious and marital aggressions that spring from Tony Weller's widder-hating humour. The

86

Wellers provide Dickens with the satirical point of view within the novel, a norm that his comedy was always to need.

Before the Wellers' entry, the comedy lacks focus. It is initially concerned with the farcical exposure of Pickwick, Tupman, Snodgrass, and Winkle, for the book begins, as everyone knows, as a comedy of humours. And the beginning is quite promising, though the promise shown in Chapter i is soon to fade. We meet the comic humours of the Pickwick Club, with Pickwick as the scientist *gloriosus*, 'the man who had traced to their source the mighty ponds of Hampstead, and agitated the scientific world with his Theory of Tittlebats', Tupman as the lover *gloriosus*, 'who to the wisdom and experience of maturer years superadded the enthusiasm and ardour of a boy, in the most interesting and pardonable of human weaknesses —love', Snodgrass as the poet *gloriosus*, and Winkle as the sportsman *gloriosus*. In Chapter ii the comic action begins, with the innocent knowledge-seeking Pickwickians on the one side, and the poker-faced lying cabbie with the forty-two-year-old horse on the other. The formula of knowledge mocking innocence is repeated very successfully several times, but far too many of the comic scenes lack tension and point. Take, for instance, the comic actions developing from the grandiose humours of the Pickwickians, the exposures of the variations on theme and situation of *homo gloriosus*. To begin with, the Pickwickians are only very weakly boastful. Pickwick can be the object of some mild jokes because as a scientist he is clearly so gullible and out of touch, but he is never really taken down because he never really aspires. This lack of comic potential in the humours shows itself all the way through. Tupman and Snodgrass are indeed scarcely developed, and though Dickens gives us a few hyperbolic bursts from Snodgrass and allows Tupman to appear at the ball, their roles are those of spectators, their humours appreciative rather than even pretentiously creative. Compare Snodgrass with Dickens's sketch of The Poetical Young Gentleman in *Sketches of Young Gentlemen* and it should be plain that in *Pickwick Papers* Dickens was not interested in developing his humours in action. The most fully deployed case of boast and exposure is Winkle, who does aspire to the sportsman's life, as a duellist, a shot, a horseman, and a skater, but he too is insufficiently vainglorious and his deflation lacks point, tension, and climax. He is led into the duel by accident rather than characteristic boast and pretence, and the episode dies away as Dr Slammer recognizes him as the wrong man and says, 'I honour your gallantry', while we look round for the joke. The same lack of contrast and tension can be found in the episode where the gallant Pickwickians are nearly run down by the army, which weakly tails off into Pickwick's hat-chase. The Pickwickians and the unwilling horse, Winkle with a gun, Pickwick and the ancient stone, Pickwick in the wrong bedroom, Winkle and Pickwick on the ice—in all these comic scenes there is very little beyond an opportunity for the illustrator. *The Middle-Aged Lady in the Double-Bedded Room* is a compressed and very funny visual version of a rather long and flat joke in words— the contrast between words and picture and the advantage of the picture brings out Lessing's pregnant

moment rather well. Even Pickwick on the ice is transformed from a hearty but pointless little episode to a
visual joke, and in this case it is not so much that the
picture makes the joke more economically but that it
makes the joke that is simply not present at all in the
text. This kind of comparison need not be laboured: it
is an interesting exercise for anyone provided with
the text and the illustrations and an interest in Dickensian humour. When a joke in *Pickwick Papers* seems
especially tedious and flat it often turns out to have some
justification in an illustration, and this is true throughout the novel, despite the dominance of Dickens's text
over the engravings of 'Phiz'.

I do not suggest that this dependence on the visual
wholly explains the weakness of much of the humour,
but rather that it makes it plain. Dickens's failing in
this novel is a weakness in farce: his spills and upsets are
physically amusing when visually rendered, but lack the
tension and character-point which are essential to farce
in fiction, and customary in the best stage farce. In Ben
Jonson, one of Dickens's important influences, it is
essential that pretentiousness and vaingloriousness
should be upset and punished. In Dickens, the physical
upset itself is all we have, and the moral humours which
are marked in Chapter i never come to anything. A fat
man on the ice, legs carefully apart, makes a funny
picture. So does a round face, topped by a nightcap,
looking out from bedcurtains while a thin lady makes
a complacent and blissfully ignorant toilet. Spread out
in words, neither joke is strong, and such jokes take up
too much space in *Pickwick Papers*. Moreover, if we
compare not only the watery humours but the farce

itself with the physical comedy in Jonson and in the eighteenth-century novel, that other marked influence on Dickens, the farce is a very mild affair, lacking the violence and exuberance of Fielding or Smollett. None of the exposures or spills are threatening, and though it is important that farce should stop short of pain and brutality, it needs to get closer to it than it does in *Pickwick Papers*. The mild humours suffer only a mild exposure. The Pickwick Club and Dingley Dell are enclosed in a magic circle and bear a charmed life.

But what about Mrs Bardell and Pickwick in the Fleet? Does not the action for breach of promise and Pickwick's imprisonment represent a breaking of the charm and the intrusion of the real world? It is true that Pickwick's innocence is slightly eroded in the Fleet, but if we look closely at these parts of the story, we find it is a restricted erosion. Pickwick sees the filth and poverty and misery which up to now he has only read about, in the stories of the Dismal Man, and other manuscripts, but the Pickwickian innocence and generosity and faith meet appropriate materials, not a challenge. Pickwick and his friends go on eating in their private room, for one of the lessons he learns is that money can buy in prison what it can buy outside. Dickens was to make a similar point in a more subtle fashion in *Little Dorrit*. Moreover, he was to confront self-indulgence with poverty: in *Bleak House* and *Great Expectations* the moral edge of the contrast between luxury and want is never blunted as it is in *Pickwick Papers*, where we meet starvation and poverty in story after story until we come to the Fleet, where the Pickwickians go on eating and drinking. Sometimes an excessive appetite for food and drink is criticized, as in the Drinking Dissenters, but the point here seems to be that we may criticize the self-indulgence of self-proclaimed Puritans while approving of the healthy appetites of those who never pretend to asceticism. We may laugh while Pickwick and his friends stagger back to Dingley Dell, a little under the influence, but there is never any moral bridge that takes us from the well-fed fat old men to the starvation that we can see in those miserably incised faces. True, Pickwick shares his food and feeds the hungry. He does it with Jingle and Job Trotter in the Fleet, but we never feel the subtler moral point of *Bleak House* or *Great Expectations*, where there is true imaginative continuity, and disease can move from poor to rich while food can stick in the throats of those who see starvation. It is not a crude matter of the characters' awareness—no one expects Pickwick to grow thin out of sympathy with the starving—but a more refined matter of the author's awareness. Can we celebrate the eating and the drinking so cheerily on the one hand and feel want so sharply on the other? The stories are cut off from the main characters and actions, and Dickens seems to exploit the segregation by placing misery in the inset tales and celebrating plenty in the main stream of action, but the contrast and juxtapositions are plainly set before the reader. And after a while the division breaks down, and Pickwick finds himself in the Fleet, no longer a reader of dismal tales but a neighbour to distress. Does Dickens show any change? After one of the Dismal Man's stories he is on the brink of telling us what Pickwick's reaction was, but interrupts himself. He never lets us into the secret.

The innocence of Pickwick is maintained to the last. Even in the Fleet he bears a charmed life. Jingle is there to be fed, to be grateful, to be converted. Dickens's optimism, his own innocence, protects his hero and makes the fable superficial. The moral enlargement of Pickwick is too cheaply purchased.

But isn't this taking the novel too seriously? My point is that the novel has indeed been taken too seriously, and if we follow up the moral interpretations closely and logically, it falls apart under the strain of such inappropriate investigation. As Pickwick says, if he does but little good, he does less harm, and his adventures are 'amusing and pleasant'. Let us take them for what they are, and drop the Christian allegory. It raises uncomfortable questions, questions that late Dickens can stand up to, but that *Pickwick Papers* cannot. It will not do to say that the macabre underworld of the novel shows Dickens's realization of want and misery: one might perhaps allow that the dark episodes subsidize the pleasant and amusing comedy. The nasty things are sealed off in separate compartments. This fragmented form is that in which Dickens could show at the same time a society he hated and feared and individual possibilities he wished to praise.

Is it possible to take Dickens's pleasant and amusing adventures in their cheery insulation? Pickwick and the Pickwickians go on eating and drinking. Since Dickens can on occasion shrink from the callousness of gluttony, in the medical students who devour meat while discussing dissection, in Stiggins and his rum, in Eatanswill itself, why does he compulsively celebrate the huge meals, accumulate the 295 references to food and drink?

Mere addition gives no idea of the quality of his celebration. It includes a loving tolerance when the right people get drunk—' "Cricket dinner—glorious party—capital songs—old port—claret—good—very good—wine, ma'am—wine." "It wasn't the wine," murmured Mr Snodgrass in a broken voice, "It was the salmon." ' It rises to a sentimental praise on occasions of Christmas, picnics, and weddings, when eating and drinking need not be merely tolerated but must be loudly applauded. Dickens is making a point, often in domestic and pastoral contexts, about gusto and *bonhomie*, about feasts and parties. He is correlating good eating and drinking with the right kind of red-blooded, full life.

He is also doing something else. David Copperfield assures us that when he imagined himself as Tom Jones, it was as 'a child's Tom Jones'. *Pickwick Papers* is a child's *Tom Jones*, too, and betrays both censorship and compensation. It is certainly not a novel without a love-interest. The comic adventures of Tupman (despite his name) and Pickwick (despite his) are anaesthetically celibate: never was a bedroom scene so determinedly and successfully innocent as that in which Pickwick gets into bed in the wrong room. And the misunderstanding with Mrs Bardell depends on our assumption that Pickwick could never really be discussing marriage or contemplating it. This does not mean—of course—that the novel lacked sexual interest. The twentieth-century reader is in no position to be impressed by the innuendoes and daring small naughtinesses of double-bedded rooms and nightcaps. We have to reduce the scale and shift the proportions.

93

Victorian pornography was a minority culture, and the majority had to take suggestiveness and arch winks and nods, and take it a very long way indeed, as it seems to us. Victorian comedy, music-hall, and fairings all reveal a consistent mild vulgarity. It may strike us that there is a huge gulf separating 'what the butler saw' from the best and worst of modern sensationalism, but the fact of such a gulf does not mean that the mild peephole joke can never be exciting. It seems to be a matter of the degree of licence and the measure of inhibition. The more inhibited your literature, the lower the threshold of sexual suggestion. Dickens had to change one of the songs he wrote for *The Village Coquette* (1836), and substitute 'A winter's night has its delight/Around old stories go' for the suggestive, 'A winter's night has its delight/Well warmed to bed we go'. The erotic threshold was lower.

Dickens seems to have been driven to celebrate some aspects of sensuous gusto, despite the moral dubiety of having so much eating and swilling in a novel concerned with want and poverty. The savage farce of the eighteenth-century picaresque novel becomes the mild antics of the Pickwickians in the field and on the ice, and the sexuality of Fielding and Smollett becomes transformed and softened too. I say 'becomes transformed' rather than 'disappears', because I think the sexual inhibition may well explain the great stress laid on eating and swilling. The Pickwickians cannot be presented as truly comic characters, cannot celebrate Dionysus, but they can get as far as the table, and are indeed seldom far from it. There is, moreover, something more tangible than a negative possibility in the figure of the

94

Fat Boy, a kind of parody of Pickwick himself. With the Fat Boy Dickens seems to bring out the proximity of sex and eating. The Fat Boy's attitudes to eating and drinking are introduced in unmistakable imagery. He 'leered horribly upon the food', and 'was hanging fondly over a capon', and bestowed 'an ardent gaze upon its plumpness'. Later on, he moves out of his eating humour and becomes amorous, but his admiration for Mary is merged with his admiration for his food, and Mary certainly sees the point: 'There was enough of the cannibal in the young gentleman's eyes to render the compliment a double one.' He goes on sighing and stuffing, occasionally coming up for speech from the pie to express a pretty ambiguous view of love, 'how we should have enjoyed ourselves at meals'. The courtship is dietetic rather than erotic. The joke is a betrayal rather than an entirely controlled example of humour. There is no need to psychoanalyse in order to observe the interest of the scene and its possible connection with the unerotic eating and drinking elsewhere in *Pickwick Papers*. Dickens can only celebrate the flesh in an inhibited and veiled way; food and drink have to suggest the carnal joviality of comedy. And the inhibition points not merely to the social responsiveness and restrictedness of this and much Victorian comedy, but also to the nature of Mr Pickwick's innocence. It is difficult to compare it with the innocence of Adam or of Don Quixote unless one has a Wellerian sense of the ill-fitting analogy.

The comedy is insulated from the harsh glimpses of real life, and in more ways than one. But is *Pickwick Papers* no more than a soft-hearted and soft-headed

novel? It takes considerable spirit to offset the sentimentality and evasiveness of the Pickwick Club and
Dingley Dell, but the novel has spirit. It has a brilliant,
hard, and fluent comic spirit, not only the comedy of
its sharp and exuberant satire but the comedy of
anecdote, farce filtered through the blandness of
Jingle, Sam Weller, and Tony Weller. It has the comic
spirit of these marvellous jokers, a comedy of character
as well as language.

What is unusual about *Pickwick Papers* as a comic
novel is that its comedy is so dependent on jokes. Its
satire it has in common with the other novels, but its
joking is all its own. Dickens's later novels are also to
dazzle us with many local spurts of fun, from the zany
stories of Mrs Gamp to the comic dialogue of Podsnap
and the foreign gentleman. Sometimes the fun is
directly connected with the theme, as in the Podsnap
instance, sometimes not, as with Mrs Gamp and
Pecksniff's idea of a wooden leg, but it is always
embedded in a comic action. In *Pickwick Papers* the
local jokes proliferate, and are at their most characteristic in the mixture of the comic and the macabre
which I spoke of earlier. It is as if the extreme segregation of soft comedy and crude pathos in the novel is
compensated for in a violent yoking together of pain
and laughter. This yoking appears in the satiric scenes
but also in the jokes. The humour of *Pickwick Papers*
comes very close to what we call sick humour. Our age
is inhibited too, in the response to pain and death, if not
in the response to sex, and it may be that the sick joke
is a characteristic feature of extreme social inhibition.
The jokes in *Pickwick Papers* well up to defy—and yet to

endorse and permit—the incredible optimism and blandness and softness of those moral conversions and arch loves in which nothing real ever happens. We have the unrealities of the loves of Winkle and Arabella, but also the violent laughter when marriage drives the man to convert himself into sausages. We have the unrealities of Pickwick and his friends in the Fleet, and the sick jokes about poverty and despair: 'There's nothin' so refreshin' as sleep, sir, as the servant-girl said afore she drank the egg-cupful o' laudanum.' There is Pickwick's sentimental celibacy set against those dreadful tales of family wretchedness and Jingle's mad anecdote about the mother's head knocked off under the arch: 'Head of a family off'. Not all the jokes are sick, of course, and the instances I give have to be seen in the context of more frivolous anecdotes, 'What the devil do you want with me, as the man said wen he see the ghost?' and 'He wants you particklar; and no one else'll do, as the Devil's private secretary said ven he fetched avay Doctor Faustus.' The brief anecdotes are as characteristic of Sam as the telegraphese is of Jingle, and both depend on the ruthless poker-faced delivery of the professional comedian, which Earle Davis, in *The Flint and the Flame* (London, 1964), has traced to its real theatrical origins. But the comedy does not depend on such compression alone, and some of the best jokes are much longer. There are the three marvellous set-pieces told by Sam: the story of his father's second marriage, the story of the buttons in the sausage-machine, and the story of the man who defied the doctor by eating the crumpets. The terrors of marriage, the law, the doctors, and death are all held at bay in the

97

violent jokes, the tall stories which manage to convert the threat into humour and yet, asserting the incongruity of laughing at *this*, recognize the threat as real. They are of course related to the splendid satire on the lawyer and the doctors. The jokes in *Pickwick Papers* are highly serious. They expand, beyond compressed story and beyond long anecdote, to the scene that is an enactment of a joke, very often of the same grisly materials as Sam Weller's brief analogies. Pickwick and the medical students, for instance, perform the macabre joke, and Tony Weller's reaction to the death of his second wife moves towards a joke without being too shocking. They connect also with the powerful sketches of satire which show Dickens s mastery of linguistic parody and caricature.

The effect of this localized comedy is of course not totally divorced from character. The three hard cases, Jingle and the Wellers, are given the toughness and earned irony which makes them the right tellers of these tales, though the process is a circular one, for the tales pile up to add more to our experience of Tony and Sam. Jingle disappoints, he and Trotter soften, and foreshadow the emigration and conversion of Micawber. There is perhaps a trace of softness in the way Dickens modulates Tony's feelings about his second wife, but it is cunningly done in the story (also rather tall, though meant seriously) about the second Mrs Weller's death, a story which caps all Tony's anti-woman jokes and permits him a faint hint of respect for the dead, moving into the final gravity of the last joke, 'Wot 'ud become of the undertakers vithout it, Sammy?' We should not exaggerate the toughness of the Wellers (as

98

I think Steven Marcus is inclined to do). Their admiration for Pickwick finally overcomes their perception of his helplessness. They are satirists with hearts of gold, their irony only shows in their jokes. Sam refuses to marry until it is quite convenient for his master (a feudal touch offensive to egalitarians) and Tony Weller tries to make over his wealth to Pickwick. Even the tough comedians are tinged with the prevailing soft colours. Dickens may be trying to show innocence coming into a knowledge of the real world but Dingley Dell surely triumphs in the end, and the real world is held at bay while innocence nods happily. The power of satire is segregated from the story of the Pickwick Club; *Pickwick Papers* comes to terms with the real world by transforming it, by cutting it down, by softening it, by separating the harsh from the sweet, by joking about it. Dickens is to find it increasingly difficult to deal with morality and society by such evasive strategies.

H

5 *Martin Chuzzlewit*

At this time in critical history it seems impossible to begin, as I should like to, with the assumption that most readers of Dickens will agree with John Forster Gissing, and various other critics, that *Martin Chuzzlewit* is a badly organized novel. This formal judgment is one I endorse, though I believe that it can do with careful scrutiny. What does this failure in composition amount to, and does it matter? If this really is the fabulous beast, James's large loose baggy monster ought we not to ask whether the novel cannot afford more bagginess than most other forms, and especially the comic novel, with its special functional mannerism which gives full effect to local assertions of wit and farce. Dickens's comic purposes make for a certain formal relaxation which flourishes many bright particulars, not all of which are subsumed by the central themes, and it is therefore no mere piety which makes me say that this novel, unusually disintegrated though it is, gets by on its patches of compelling gusto,[1] comic and also grim. Nevertheless, its defects of form are important, largely because they expose, in several ways some of Dickens's weaknesses of feeling and dramatic power.

[1] P. N. Furbank, in his *Penguin* edition of the novel, objects that this is a 'Philistine' term. I had not intended it as such, but had in mind Hazlitt's use and definition.

But not all readers would agree that there is a formal failure. Many of the recent interpretations by close and serious critics have claimed for *Martin Chuzzlewit* a depth and coherence of thought and feeling which makes me wonder whether I have read the same book, and before I say anything about my own views, I must look briefly at some of those strange images of Dickens—as they appear to me—so freely bred by post-Jamesian criticism. For though James rejected many nineteenth-century novels as shapeless and uneconomical, it is probably his insistence on the totally relevant narrative structure which is now partly responsible for our attempts to deny the looseness and bagginess of so many of the Victorians.

It is not a mere formal exaggeration which is at work in criticism of the novel. Several recent critics have established Dickens's formal power by trying to prove that his novels have a consistent and unified ideological structure. I can truthfully say that the *Martin Chuzzlewit* of Jack Lindsay (*Charles Dickens*, London, 1950), Dorothy Van Ghent ('The Dickens World: A View from Todgers's', *Sewanee Review*, lviii, 1950), and J. Hillis Miller (*Charles Dickens*, Cambridge, Mass. and London, 1958), is a novel—or rather, three different novels—which I should like to read. Lindsay's novel, in which the young Martin represents the adventurous enterprise of capitalism, Jonas the dark usurious exploitation, and Mark Tapley the unbreakable common man, has coherence of symbolic characterization and social analysis, though in his fine observations on Dickens's transmutation of tension and fantasy Lindsay recognizes Dickens's instability. The visions of disintegration explored by Dorothy Van Ghent and Hillis Miller, while illuminating many aspects of the work, suggest a psychological subtlety and grasp. And there is Sylvère Monod's poetic novel (*Dickens romancier*, Paris, 1953) with its beauty and gaiety—Dickens's worst flights of gassy rhetoric sound controlled and elegant in French—and Edgar Johnson's morally unified novel making the transition from gloom to warmth.

Critics like these, standing well away from the lunatic fringe, suggest the appearance of a vast parasitic growth, a super-criticism which blurs analysis in re-creation, and scarcely needs to consider judgment. I know of no Victorian novelist who has been recreated in the image of his critics so frequently and so strongly as Dickens. It is not just a matter of our current obsession with total relevance which makes us consider all the Victorians as if they were formal artists after the manner of Turgenev, Stevenson, and James himself. The interpretations I have just mentioned are ideological rather than formalist exaggerations. Dickens's combination of striking satire and animistic description tempts us to think that he must have a more coherent moral scheme than he really has. His attempts to combine a moral action with his strong static social portraiture, his vague gestures towards *Bildungsroman*—all coming in part from his lack of intellectual quality, and all particularly conspicuous in *Martin Chuzzlewit*—attract the force of more methodical and original minds.

But the critic who is wary of imposing an intellectual scheme—or who may not have one to impose—may be as guilty of free distortion as the Marxist or existentialist arguing his thematic unity. We now have ready to hand the apparently objective techniques of formal analysis, and the thematic defence of Dickens's form in *Martin Chuzzlewit* ranges from the subtle to the simple. Edgar Johnson, for instance, has this to say:

> With the exception of the rather digressive American episodes (and a little special pleading might bring even them into the pattern), all the characters are linked by their relationship to the theme of selfishness. In a curious way this rendition of a generalized vice gives *Martin Chuzzlewit* affinities with novels otherwise so different as George Meredith's *The Egoist* and Jane Austen's *Pride and Prejudice*. ... His exposure of selfishness is as sharp, if not as subtle, as Meredith's dissection of egoism, and his method is identical with Jane Austen's, whose characters are all mutations on pride and prejudice. (*Charles Dickens*)

The resemblance between these three novels is indeed peculiar, unless it is merely obvious. Dickens does state formally that he is setting out to explore the theme of selfishness, but there are a very large number of novels, and many other forms of literary and non-literary discourse, doing the same thing. I am sure it is harder to find novels which lack the unity of theme than novels which possess it. It does not distinguish the novel from other forms, nor does it distinguish the good novel from the bad. Moral unity is the unity of the writer's categories and it is only one aspect of narrative form. It need not affect the action of the novel, which usually shows these categories in a tense progression, and once we leave problems of form, of which it is only a part, it has no relevance either to the moral and psychological insight of the artist, or to his dramatic, poetic, or critical handling. To say that a novel has the unity of its moral categories is to say only one minimal thing about its structure, and is certainly to decide nothing about its merit.

The formal critic may of course use this reductive concept more critically, and relate it to the Aristotelian relations of beginning, middle, and end. This is what Edgar B. Benjamin does in his article, 'The Structure of *Martin Chuzzlewit*', *Philological Quarterly*, xxxiv (1955). He looks at moral unity in terms of formal progression, interpreting the main humour as Hypocrisy, and describing the structure in terms of Hypocrisy's rise and fall: Hypocrisy Ascendant, Triumphant, and Unmasked. But his attention to action, I think, is only specious: he picks out the changes in the situation of hypocritical characters but seems to assume that these changes, and their exemplary significance, determines the movement of tension in the novel. This is something which I doubt.

We cannot—especially in Dickens—make an automatic correlation between moral change and narrative action. I would of course agree that the characters have this extensive moral commitment to the general theme of selfishness and often to the more specialized variant of hypocrisy. The comic characters (the Pecksniff family, Mrs Gamp, the Moulds) express the theme in their personal, professional, and social roles; the grimmer characters (Jonas and Tigg Montague) do the same. And there are a few characters (old Martin, young Martin, and Mercy Chuzzlewit, with the possible additions of Tom Pinch and Mark Tapley) who may be said to undergo some change in their attitude to their own or other people's preoccupation with Self. Some of the changes in the novel involve the delineation of a change of heart, others seem to involve the change from a comic to a serious mode. Action which depends on a change of heart is plainly an example of tension provided by moral interest, and if we pick some obvious examples of novels having this kind of moral action we might add *Great Expectations* and *Hard Times* to a list including *Emma*, *Middlemarch*, and *The Ambassadors*. The problem of moral action in Dickens's work as a whole I have already discussed and I want to make it clear that what I see as the gap between moral theme and action in *Martin Chuzzlewit* is not a dislocation invariably characteristic of Dickens. Dickens is concerned with showing moral change: how does he do it? We need to ask further questions too. How far are the tensions, expectations, and surprises which make the curve of our attention—the line of action—concerned with the moral subject?

The action is concerned with moral causality: it is in part at least precipitated by the theme of Self. The impersonations of the elder Chuzzlewit, the exiles of Martin, Mark Tapley, Tom Pinch, the attempted murder of Anthony Chuzzlewit, and the actual murder of Tigg Montague, the speculator and blackmailer, are all caused by selfishness, unselfishness, or by the desire to test, expose and reform selfishness and unselfishness. Selfishness is also given its forms of Nemesis, including the public Jonsonian exposure of Pecksniff's deceit and hubris, the punishment of Mercy in her marriage to Jonas, the ordeal of Martin in Eden, and the stern advice given to Mrs Gamp. On the credit side there are the rewards of Tom, Ruth, John Westlock, Mark

Tapley, and the young Martin. The theme expresses itself actively—apart from the content of character—in the demonstration of a change of heart and in this use of moral cause and effect. But how much of our reading interest depends on this moral significance? And how is the moral action handled, and with what conviction and plausibility? I should like to try to answer both questions together.

The only important part of the action which runs right through the novel is the impersonation of Old Chuzzlewit, and its consequences in the duping of Pecksniff and the exile of Martin. It provides some mystery, some irony, and some scenes which enact the humours. There is the hypocritical domestic show put on for Martin's benefit, several scenes of moral antithesis between young Martin and Tom Pinch, the splendid quarrel scene in which the predatory Chuzzlewit hypocrites fall out, the scene where Old Chuzzlewit lies to Pecksniff while Pecksniff is lying to him. Such scenes are frequent at the beginning, then thin out, and reappear in a conspicuous huddle towards the end when we have the revelation of Martin's trick, the exposure of Pecksniff, and the general apportionment of rewards and punishments. This one over-arching piece of action does indeed over-arch. It is important at the beginning and end but stays more or less out of sight for a large part of the novel; and when it does appear it is markedly unproductive of tension. There are indeed so few rising intonations of curiosity, doubt, and expectation at the beginning of the novel that it is not surprising that the novel was not a success as a serial, though no doubt all the other reasons which have been suggested for this relative failure—disappointment with *Barnaby Rudge*, reviewers' hostility to *American Notes*, the change to monthly publication, harshness of satire, lack of pathetic children and deaths —may also be important. But the striking difference between this novel and almost all Dickens's others is this absence of initial tension. Most of the others create a rising curve of attention, and do this, I think, by presenting at the beginning both strong incident and some point of emotional identification. Incident and human emotional centre are both present, for instance, in the death of Mrs Dombey, the mystery of Esther's birth, Pip's encounter with Magwitch, the first river scene in *Our Mutual Friend*. Sometimes the incident alone is arresting, as in the workhouse scene in the first chapter of *Oliver Twist*, sometimes the introductory scene is symbolic, as in *Bleak House* and *Little Dorrit*, but in all these novels we also move swiftly forward to a strong human identification. Leaving aside the tiresome exercise in sarcasm which is the prelude to Martin Chuzzlewit—its focus now seems blurred—there is no exciting incident in the early chapters. There are indeed very few strongly exciting situations anywhere in the novel, apart from Martin's trip to Eden and the criminal career of Jonas Chuzzlewit—and neither of these sources of tension is anticipated by any early trailers. The human centre is missing too: the most interesting and conspicuous character is Pecksniff and he is as useless for purposes of identification as Micawber, presented as he is from the outside, and in a strong harsh stereotype. Martin is too neutral and uninteresting, and is also scarcely ever seen from the inside, at least until his traumatic experiences. The one character whose emotions are dramatized with any strength is Tom Pinch, and he is not only a grossly sentimental figure but is also given practically nothing to do. In these three characters, as they appear, there seems to be no potentiality for either tense action or emotional identification, but the wasted opportunity lies in the conflict and impersonation of old Martin. This impersonation is neither prominent nor made productive of much mystery, influence, or dramatic irony—the comparison with the brilliant impersonation of Boffin's miserly humour in *Our Mutual Friend*, which is mysterious, affects other characters, and is rich in irony and innuendo, should make this clear. Boffin's assumed humour is motivated—engineered by Harmon for the cure of Bella. It is influential—it does cure her. And as an impersonation it is like Malcolm's in *Macbeth* and provides a special exaggerated moral symbol of the prevailing evil in the novel. Martin's impersonation is much more weakly motivated, and has barely more than a concluding pantomimic resolution in action.

If the moral content does not terminate in action, as I am arguing, what then constitutes the incident of the early parts of the novel? There are brilliant comic scenes with a great deal of satire, linguistic humour, and farce. But although these scenes usually have thematic relevance they seldom move—and why should they?—beyond a self-contained action which raises no questions and leaves no disturbing loose ends. There is certainly some attempt at the moral conflict which in other novels produces its tension, in personal relationships which have a moral antithesis: Nicholas and Smike, Dombey and Florence, Hexam and Lizzie, and so on. But the moral antithesis in *Martin Chuzzlewit* strikes me as purely formal. There is the moral opposition of old Martin and Pecksniff, of young Martin first with Tom Pinch, then with Mark Tapley. None of these morally significant pairs is shown in the tension of personal relation—there is no human antagonism, or love, or fear, or any of the conflicting emotions which mark the relations of Oliver and Fagin, or Pip and Magwitch, or Florence and Dombey, where the moral antithesis is expressed in human relations, and changes accordingly. The only parts of *Martin Chuzzlewit* which show a personal as well as a moral conflict are either presented offstage in exposition, like the relationship between Martin and his grandfather, which is potentially of the same mixed human and moral tension as these examples from the better novels, or are not primarily explored for moral antithesis. Mercy's relation to the sadistic Jonas with its pleas and cries on behalf of outraged sacred womanhood, or the relation of Mary Graham to Pecksniff in his role of repulsive furtive lecher, are not moving as *moral* dramatizations.

It might be argued that although Martin started off as a neutral character, he does come to provide a point of identification: he is the only character shown in the process of change. Dickens nearly always makes his gestures to *Bildungsroman*, and *Hard Times* and *Great Expectations*—I am not so sure about *Our Mutual Friend* —make much more than gestures, in his Jacobean mode of conventionalized psychology. Martin's need for change is shown right at the beginning, but when the change comes it is segregated from the rest of the action, both in place and in effect. Martin's conversion is made visible only to Mark Tapley, in Eden. It does up to a point constitute a self-contained action with a beginning, middle, and end: Martin's is the responsibility for going to America and then to Eden, though the moral weakness which emerges here is impetuous innocence rather than selfishness. It is followed by his climactic vision of Self, after sickness, disillusion, and admiration for Mark, his moral opposite, and culminates in the triumphant affirmation of some belief in America's possible Phoenix-like rebirth. But this account of the action, like Benjamin's account of the rise and fall of hypocrisy, is misleading because it ignores the method of presentation. Action is implied rather than drama-tized in this moral change, and although the abruptness, the crisis, and the use of external example in Mark, are characteristic of many of Dickens's sudden conversions, the absence of any sense of time is particularly noticeable in this novel because of the general superficial treatment of Martin's moral conduct. Dickens tells us that the change of heart did not come about in a moment, but this is telling, not showing,[1] and the process of months jammed into a few paragraphs with no correlative for the passage of time:

It was natural for him to reflect—he had months to do it in—upon his own escape, and Mark's extremity. This led him to consider which of them could be the better spared, and why? Then the curtain slowly rose a very little way; and Self, Self, Self, was shown below ... It was long before he fixed the knowledge of himself so firmly in his mind that he could thoroughly

[1] I have decided to leave the repetition of some discussion already included in Chapter 2, rather than truncate the argument in either chapter.

discern the truth; but in the hideous solitude of that most hideous place, with Hope so far removed, Ambition quenched, and Death beside him rattling at the very door, reflection came, as in a plague-beleaguered town; and so he felt and knew the failing of his life, and saw distinctly what an ugly spot it was. (ch. xxx)

The suddenness is common, as I say, and there is no point in comparing Dickens's conversions again with the slow and often eddying movement traced in George Eliot or Henry James. But I think this change is even more abrupt in exposition, relying heavily on compressed rhetoric, than the fairly abrupt conversions of David Copperfield or Bella Wilfer, though the important difference lies in the context of dramatized moral action. Dombey, Steerforth, Gradgrind, Pip, and other major and minor examples of flawed character—not necessarily changing—are demonstrated in appropriate action, large and small. Steerforth, for instance, is not given only the decisive action of seducing Emily, but various other significant acts of selfishness—baiting the poor usher, making David read to him at night, and so on. Martin's violent change appears in a very different context of action, for Martin is given very little to do. His selfishness, like his grandfather's, is shown in exposition in the moral contrasts I have mentioned and in a series of trivial physical gestures which are closer to theatrical business than to dramatic action: twice he keeps the fire from Tom, once he lets Tom carry his greatcoat. Small details like this have a place in moral delineation, but here they carry too large a load.

Martin's selfishness is also motivated, showing Dickens's interest in environment and heredity, but the origins like the effects are also presented in exposition, in contrast with, say, *David Copperfield* or *Great Expectations*. And his actions as a changed man are again expressed mainly at the level of business—he surprises Mark by expressing sympathy for Tom, he rebukes Mark for staying on the windy side instead of taking turn and turn about. There is no active effect. When Pip and David change there are repercussions throughout all their relationships. But the inconspicuous relation between Mary and Martin is totally unaffected by his change, and so indeed is his relation to his grandfather. Although his admissions of wrong and change are made at the end, he is a passive figure. It would not be true to say that he is always passive: in his role as lover and as a selfish man undergoing change he is given inadequate expression in action, but he has a very important role in the American episodes. But there is something a little odd here: although America provides the test and ordeal, the sense of responsibility, and the endurance, there is no visible relation between Martin's selfishness and the dramatization on a national scale of the hypocritical and aggressive selfishness of America. His main role here, as he is lionized like his creator, is to act as spirited and zealous critic of America, given the *ex officio* wisdom and objectivity of his Englishness. There is indeed, as we all know, this thematic connection between the social satire and the individual types of selfishness, but it is worth observing that Dickens makes no dramatic acknowledgement of the resemblance in the presentation of Martin. He temporarily drops his humour and is as human and zealous as Mark. It shows the superficial and imposed nature of his selfish humour, and shows too a dislocation characteristic of this novel.

The third important part of the action is of course the blackmail and murder. Percy Lubbock, who writes all too briefly in *The Craft of Fiction* about Dickens, observes that in all the novels except *David Copperfield* it is 'his chosen intrigue, his "plot" that makes the shape of his book', and although I think this is a simplification which ignores Dickens's use of contrast and cross-cutting, the formal 'streaky bacon' as he calls it in *Oliver Twist*, it is a sound comment which once more emphasizes the importance of action. It is true that the intrigue, the sensational and intricate web of plotting and mystery, usually occupies only a part of the formula in a Dickens novel. The usual formula is made up of this kind of plot, and some moral process, a love-story or two, and a specialized social satire, not to mention the more or less connected comic scenes. In the late novels, from *Bleak House* onwards, the plot is inextricably related, in symbolism and causality, to all the other narrative elements, and it seems to be true—in one sense at least—that the tensions and expectations of the intrigue 'give shape'. They compensate for the lack of continuous moral or psychological action and for the essentially static and self-contained nature of most of the satiric and comic action—some parts of *David Copperfield* and *Great Expectations* strongly excepted. In *Martin Chuzzlewit* the only tense and dynamic action starts too late to have this kind of total structural compensation. It is presented in a chunk, rather like the American episode, though interwoven of course with all the other pieces of what I hesitate to call action. Jonas's story is a well-handled exercise in the manner of Poe: a study in the psychology of guilt, fear, and the perverse imp that tempts to self-exposure. It has small beginnings in Jonas's aggressiveness to his father, and in his threat after the proposal, then moves mysteriously through the death of Anthony, the blackmail of Tigg Montague, his murder, and culminates in one of the best unmasking scenes in Dickens, with the brilliant use of Mrs Gamp, for once trembling with more than gin, and the comic-sinister announcement of the actual appearance of Mrs Harris. It is not as various and subtle as the analysis of the passions of Bill Sikes or Bradley Headstone, but it exposes its limited passions with hallucinatory power: Montague's fear of the door, Jonas's fear of the locked room, his beating heart, and his telltale face. (*The Telltale Heart* was published in January 1841, the month when the publication of *Martin Chuzzlewit* began, and though I know of no evidence that Dickens read it, there seems to me to be as striking a resemblance between the Jonas parts and Poe's story as between that story and its supposed Dickens source in *The Clockcase*—a nice case, if true, of a source with its tail in its mouth.) The criminal psychology is finely done, and so too is the revelation of the card up the author's sleeve. Jonas discovers that he has not really killed his father and so need not have killed Montague, and the combination of expectation and surprise here is worthy of the more dexterous double trick pulled off in *Our Mutual Friend* (the novel for which *Martin Chuzzlewit* acts as a source in several ways). This part of the action has also been described as thematically insistent: here is selfishness carried to the extreme of murder, and though I do not think that the excitement and tension are dependent upon this moral significance, it is true that selfishness precipitates the action. This is not re-markable—murder is rarely selfless. The theme fits where it touches, and I would have thought that what engages our interest—what is central—is the psychology of crime and punishment rather than the anatomy of selfishness.

There is another way, apart from the mechanical unifying source of family relations, in which this action is related to the rest of the novel. Jonas is shown as the sadistic husband of poor transformed Mercy/Merry Chuzzlewit. If one of the formal characteristics of this novel is the lack of integrating action, another is surely a very characteristic lack of continuity in character. Is there any other novel where the characters are so made over for new roles? Mercy and—to some extent—Jonas seem to begin as comic characters, and become players in the grim melodrama. Montague Tigg becomes Tigg Montague. Chevy Slyme becomes a policeman. Bailey of Todgers's becomes the boy who travels with Jonas and Montague, who is believed dead, and who is joy-fully resurrected at the end. Jonas is perhaps the only successful example—he moves quite convincingly from mean and furtive aggressiveness to large predatoriness and brutality, and there is no difficulty about moving from his outside to the inner point of view: it is the same technique Dickens used earlier with Bill Sikes. Apart from *David Copperfield* and *Great Expectations*, Dickens's psychology is most convincing when he is dramatizing sensations of guilt, fear, and panic. Mercy, Tigg, Bailey, and Chevy are each merely two charac-ters joined by being given the same name: there are the bridging explanations that Mercy is getting her punishment for her frivolity, that Tigg was given the money by old Martin to start him off in large speculation, that Chevy is still resentful at having to take on a job unworthy of his powers, but these are imposed. Bailey as the comic boy of Todgers—'There's a fish tomorrow. Just come. Don't eat none of him!'—bears no resemblance to the pathetic boy who is merely a silent dummy used to arouse pity and fear. The use of Mrs Gamp in the *dénouement* is the most successful example of Dickens's habit of making a character do overtime, and here there is not only the careful preparation in Betsy Prig's terrible attack on the substantiality of Mrs Harris—'I don't believe there's no sich a person'—but also a certain turn of the screw in the melodramatic use of the invisible comic alter ego. These are instances of loose ends being so carefully tucked into the wrong place that their looseness, and their mechanical structure, is revealed. Dickens is both careful and slap-happy about some aspects of composition: there is indeed a good passage where he seems to be parodying and anticipating certain excesses of thematic analysis:

From Mr Moddle to Eden is an easy and natural transition. Mr Moddle, living the atmosphere of Miss Pecksniff's love, dwelt (if he had but known it) in a terrestrial Paradise. The thriving city of Eden was also a terrestrial Paradise, upon the showing of its proprietors. The beautiful Miss Pecksniff might have been poetically described as a something too good for man in his fallen and degraded state. That was exactly the character of the thriving city of Eden... (ch. xxxiii)

Dickens's transitions, in this novel and in others, are handled in a variety of ways. This example is characteristic of a certain mechanical composition which often derives from a relationship of theme but very seldom from a continuity of feeling. The transitions in character are managed with a similar superimposition of theoretical relation: Mercy is both changed and punished by her marriage, Tigg becomes Montague—with a drastic linguistic change and a similarly imposed explanation after the fact. What really seems to happen is that Dickens switches from the comic to the melodramatic mode: there is a purely intellectual movement made possible—though we cannot do more than guess about the causality—by the absence of what Coleridge called the unity of feeling. Form and psychology cannot be divorced: the difference between George Eliot's transitions from Dorothea to Casaubon, and Dickens's from Eden to Moddle, or between the thematic unity of characters like Lydgate and Raffles, and characters like Martin and Pecksniff and Mrs Honimy, is that George Eliot's unity is one of feeling: her characters are conceived imaginatively as made out of the same relation to environment, the same aspirations, fantasies, and selfish and selfless urges. Dickens moves from one mode to another, and sometimes makes his connections work in theme rather than action.

At times they do not work. His tidiness may be plausible, as in his final use of Mrs Gamp, or may be tolerated though implausible, as in the exploitation of Bailey as the pathetic child-figure for which he is scarcely qualified by his earlier appearances. But at times there are glaring examples of contradictions left unreconciled, or of resemblances of which Dickens seems unaware. One of these is Martin's dual role as

selfish man and critic of selfishness. Another is the conspicuous transition from the satirical use of hyperbole
and rhetorical question and metaphor in Pecksniff and
the totally uncritical linguistic extravagance of Tom
Pinch. Consider the very last juxtaposition in the novel.
In the last chapter we have Moddle's very funny flight
from the altar—'Unalterably, never yours, Augustus'
—and then immediately afterwards comes the last bid
for pathos in Tom Pinch's equally romantic un-
requited longings for Another who is Another's.
Pecksniff's exaggerations are a correlative for insincerity,
Dickens's exaggerations on behalf of Tom are in deadly
earnest, and here coincidence shows the lack of imaginative comparison and judgment of emotion and style.
The great satirist can turn to gross sentimentality without his left hand knowing what his right hand is doing.
The content of Moddle's yearnings and isolation come
unhappily before the final full-blast appeal from Tom's
plight: Moddle's 'e'en now' and the author's 'Thou
wert by her side' to Tom, are dangerously close, and
Moddle's comic 'Unalterably' changes to the ecstatic
vision of final reunion in Heaven. The differences are
as revealing as the resemblances: Moddle's farewell is
studded with bathos: '300 tons per register—forgive
me if in my distraction I allude to the ship', whereas
our farewell to Tom plays on the associations of religion,
gardens, music, and—of course—children. There are
no major death-beds and pathetic children in the novel,
but Dickens deliberately used—or felt intensely—
their powerful appeal when he introduced Mary's child,
who is significantly 'slight' and (on one occasion, calling
for Tom to be her patient nurse) on á sick-bed. The *vox*

humana of the pathetic mode and the comic exaggeration of its opposite are good examples of Dickens's formal completion and fundamental failure to connect. The result is unintentional self-parody.

The acceptability of the Dickensian sensibility, and its relation both to his sense of audience and his private fantasy, is still a problem: we mostly agree with Oscar Wilde that one must have a heart of stone not to laugh at Little Nell, but we still disagree about Paul Dombey. But admitting the variability of individual thresholds of sensibility and taste, I should like to suggest the relevance of formal analysis to this question of Dickens's emotional taste. In the first chapter of *Oliver Twist* there is the death-bed and the birth, with the theatrical rhetoric of 'Let me see the child and die'. Out of context this may seem regrettable, but in the context the pathos is not only contrasted with the institutional satire of workhouse officialdom, but rooted in it: the mother is unparticularized but the matter-of-factness of the doctor and the beery old women gives the situation a particular reason for its pathos. Another example comes from *Dombey and Son*. When Paul tells Toots about the wild waves there is the particularity and contrast of the two odd, not to say touched, children, one babbling his sick vision, the other with his practical obtuse inability to share it. This may be in part a matter of aesthetic distance, but I believe it is mainly a matter of particularity. Intense emotional appeal, in realistic arts like fiction and drama, may well need the particularity of social situation and human contrast. The workhouse doctor and Toots act rather like the Nurse in *Romeo and Juliet*, and reveal both the rareness of the intensity and the solid human habitation from which it springs. The separation of the comic, pathetic, and melodramatic modes in *Martin Chuzzlewit* means that this constant checking and solidfying of pathos very seldom takes place. And the novel acts as a self-made analysis of Dickens's defects of archness and pathos, exposing them in their nakedness, and showing by contrast how he so often manages the same emotional appeal in a way which comes off in other novels.

On the whole, the comedy has nothing to say to the arch love-story of Ruth and John or to the pathos of Tom Pinch, who stands in for the innocent and pathetic child. Together with the melodrama, and surpassing it in its variety and concreteness, it is the main source of vitality in *Martin Chuzzlewit*. Its resilient and compulsive caricatures are not altered by their contact with the serious characters: Mrs Gamp is warned and Pecksniff exposed and degraded, but the two main comic characters are spared the shift of mode which disintegrates Montague Tigg, Chevy Slyme, and Bailey. The comedy provides its own special source of tension—we await the return to its self-contained comic farce and continued mannerism as the one firm line of interest in the novel. There is more and less than thematic continuity here: even Mr Pecksniff's drunken longings to see Mrs Todger's idea of a wooden leg depends in part on our recollection of his instructions to Martin to produce his idea of a monument to the Lord Mayor, or a tomb for a sheriff, or a nobleman's cowhouse, but Mrs Gamp's husband's wooden leg is, I hope, as essentially unrelated to Mrs Todgers's 'idea' as Mrs Gamp is to a White Goddess. Satire and sick humour flourish in the most influential of Dickens's comic prototypes—she is the Dogberry of syntax, the drunken nurse full of gorgeous child-bed morbidity—and there is, I hope, social realism granted, no symbolic resonance in the umbrella (*pace* Mr Miller), the cowcumber, or Mrs Harris's portrait. The farce, the brilliant lingusitic incongruity, parody, and zany oddity, on the one hand, and the harsh, unfair, splendid American satire, on the other, show a sure handling and an expansiveness which other parts of an ineffectual action sorely need.

6 *David Copperfield*

David Copperfield is a Victorian novel, and its powers and defects have to be seen in the context of its age. It is a *Bildungsroman* or novel of education, based on models neither purely nineteenth-century nor purely English. Its powers and defects spring from the character and art of its creator, and in this novel, his 'favourite child', he was keeping very close to life, and the relation between author and novel is a complex and interesting one. It is an autobiographical novel, though this term will only guide our understanding and appreciation if we use it to describe not only the obvious reporting of actual happenings and details in Dickens's life, but also its sensitive openness, not disconnected with the report of actuality, to the personal drives of dissatisfactions and desires. If it can be called autobiographical, it must also be called inventive, and its inventiveness creates a very individual emotional range, both comic and serious, which has very little to do with visible sources, contexts, and models, but which must be praised, criticized, and above all, *recognized*, as centrally and typically Dickensian. Like most works of art, it is less than perfect, and something has to be said about its unevenness.

A few words about its Victorianism. There is less explicit criticism of Victorian society in this novel than in Dickens's other writings: his eye was on his own domestic and spiritual adventures, and not on social injustice. Being the man he was, seeing his own life necessarily involved some social criticism, but this emerges implicitly, and often unconsciously. There are some exceptions. The book contains some hard nuggets of topical concern, usually extractable and conspicuous: the plea for prostitutes and their reclaim, the satire on the law, the criticism of model prisons, the interest in emigration. These mostly appear as tractlike forms within the continuum of the novel, not digressions but certainly statements in a different mode. We may feel that the treatment of Em'ly's seduction suffers from being part of a generalized case about fallen women, but we are most likely to applaud the formalized little coda about prison reform, which allows the three villains to take a final bow and create a new piece of satirical irony. But these embedded tracts are few. More typical and more interesting is the revelation of Dickens's implicit social attitudes, often remaining well below the conscious level of criticism. In Dickens's other study of psychological growth, *Great Expectations*, the psychological concerns are socially expressive: Pip's humiliations, ambitions, illusions, snobbishness, gentlemanliness, and fall and rise, are all recognizable social symbols. The novel is at once a portrait of an individual character and a strong generalization, and Dickens consciously and ironically and movingly manipulates the fusion. But in *David Copperfield*, because he is closer to his hero, and in a position where he found it hard to be distanced and objective, the relation of psychology to social expression is markedly different. David often reveals—or rather *betrays*—

123

Victorian limitations which the author does not see but which the modern reader most certainly does. David's dissatisfaction with Dora's housekeeping, for instance, is very plainly both characteristic of his sex and age, an expectation and a need which it never occurs to him to question or criticize. He takes very great pains to show David's painful attempts, after intolerant and demanding mistakes, to accept Dora as she is, and the tolerance and compromise are clearly meant to be seen as meritorious. In a sense they are, but what we, as modern readers, are likely to do is to set aside the limited assumption that every man deserves a good housekeeper, and sympathize with the undated and moving residue—David's difficult decision to accept another human being for what she is, which is not what he wants or needs. Or again, David's chief professional characteristic as an artist, in one of the strangest portraits of an artist ever written, seems to be hard work. The modern reader, associating a rather different set of values with the artist's life (whether he likes them or not does not matter), is likely to find it difficult to sympathize with this emphasis. Not that we can quite call it a Victorian concept of the artist: Wilhelm Meister, before David Copperfield, and Will Ladislaw or Hans Meyrick, after him, are quite close to the Bohemian stereotype which makes us expect the artist to be irrational, unstable, rootless, unhappy, wounded. Dickens himself fits our idea of the wounded artist with his creative bow much better than David Copperfield, but here again, we are likely to extract the Victorian admiration for industry, placed in a curious collocation, and accept the less dateable part of the portrait, that humane curiosity and shrewd observation which Dickens picks out from the very beginnings of the novel, as characteristic of David as an embryonic novelist. Such socially determined elements, of which the author is unconscious, play an interesting part in the novel, but they form only a part of it, and are happily combined with concerns and interests which can still command our sympathy.

There are some moments when Dickens seems to make the imaginative effort to move outside a socially limited obtuseness. Up to a point, we may feel superior and critical before Dickens's unsympathetic portrait of Uriah Heep, whose servility and unctuousness are plainly created by an illiberal society. But here Dickens manages devastatingly to make his hero feel the dull distaste and yet recognize the social implication: Uriah is the creature of his time, and placing the social responsibility where it belongs makes him no more likeable. Dickens is perhaps not totally able to draw the moral, though he struggles. After the last revelation of Heep's 'infamy', David speaks in terms both priggish and, I think, inaccurate:

'It may be profitable to you to reflect, in future, that never were greed and cunning in the world yet, that did not do too much, and over-reach themselves. It is as certain as death.'

To which Heep's reply, despite the moral implications of his own downfall, seems clearly the last word, in realism and social insight, after the simplifications and wish-fulfilment of David's innocence:

'Or as certain as they used to teach at school (the same school where I picked up so much umbleness), from nine o'clock to eleven, that labour was a curse, and from eleven o'clock to one, that it was a blessing and a cheerfulness, and a dignity, and I don't know what all, eh?' said he with a sneer. 'You preach about as consistent as they did. Won't umbleness go down?'

Since the novel ends with umbleness going down splendidly, albeit in prison, this riposte seems to mark a rare division between Dickens and David. It certainly marks Dickens's imaginative recognition of the social significance of Heep and the socially determined nature of the ethics of industry. Dickens is not perhaps entirely behind the comment, for he does use his art to celebrate the certainty of vice's downfall, and he does elsewhere preach the blessedness and dignity of labour pretty loudly, but the passage marks, I think, a fruitful uncertainty, a movement of the critical imagination beyond those historical limitations which operated on it. It is always dangerous to patronize Dickens's social complacency: he may not be consistently critical, but the very unpredictability with which he can jump over his own Victorian fence makes it safer to expect subtlety and insight rather than blindness.

Our response certainly does not always fulfill his expectations of sympathy and approval, though there were Victorian readers who also shrank from some of his excesses of pathos and solemnity. But there is no doubt that our tolerance of some areas of feeling, or some kinds of demands on feeling, have radically shifted. When David sees Agnes as the figure in the stained-glass window, 'pointing upward', the Excelsior effects are unlikely to come off, not just because our attitudes to women have become happily less ideal, but because Dickens is counting on a context of religious reverence to bring his readers halfway to meet him, which is likely to send a fair number of his modern readers racing off in the opposite direction. I do not think we can here attack Dickens for exploiting religiosity and counting on a too easy generalized or stock response. He may have been cold-bloodedly manipulating the reader—a dated stock response can scarcely be tested for sincerity—but it is more likely that he was quite naturally and uncritically making and expecting stock responses in a way that we all do, in creating art or in daily life. Later novelists are not necessarily more particularized and concrete in their rendering of feeling, but are drawing on expectations of different stock responses. We were, for instance, especially ready to sympathize with the inhibited stoic who fears the insincerities of the language of strong feeling. Who can doubt that Hemingway sometimes relied on the stock response to the collocation of the laconic and the nobly sincere, just as Dickens relied on the stock response which gives a double measure of feeling for the collocations of religion and woman, or woman and child? Dickens expected his readers to admire hard work, domestic efficiency, a high degree of rationality, and competence, and did not usually take the trouble to argue, objectify, or particularize such merits. James Joyce expected his readers to sympathize with outsiders, exiles, and victims of persecution, and also perhaps relied to some extent on stock responses in his creation of Leopold Bloom.

I do not suggest that our judgment should be over-ruled by the tolerant efforts of our historical imagination. I think the religious/feminine ideal presented in

Agnes is repulsive, and the childlike/feminine/sickly appeal of the dying Dora only slightly less so. We must admit the problem of the man, as well as the habits of the age. There were good biographical reasons why Dickens should tend to sentimentality when he was treating death, children, and ideal women. George Eliot is very much more tolerable on the domestic ideal (by which Mrs Poyser and Dinah pass, and Hetty fails) but tends to be lachrymose on the subjects of brother and sister and very small children. Dickens's own Mrs Bagnet in *Bleak House* is a very splendid instance of the domestic ideal, and Paul Dombey and the young David Copperfield are particularized where Little Nell is left blank, to be filled in by the stock response. *David Copperfield* is flawed by vagueness and inflated demands, but it has plenty of vivid, particular, and entirely successful demands to make on our feelings.

Take, for instance, the childhood scenes of the early parts of the novel. They are not only vivid, recapturing the closeness, sharpness, and disproportionate power and mystery of the child's sensations, but are perfectly adapted to the character-study Dickens is creating. David is a sensitive child, and his sensitivity is to make him terribly vulnerable to adult cruelty and adult neglect. It is also to make him alert and alive, with the curious observant eye of an insecurity sharpened not only by intelligence but by the inability to take any experience for granted. Dickens's psychology of childhood, so often rightly praised, must be seen as part of the psychology of the whole character, a study in isolation and the novelist's imagination. Once more, we need to admit that the novel is uneven. David can be seen as a complex thinking and feeling character, but only up to a point.

Dickens has been often praised, in recent years, for his 'episodic intensification', that power of creating strong, moving, and convincing details, moments, and scenes. Critics like Gwendolyn Needham and Edgar Johnson have praised *David Copperfield* for its powers of thematic unification and control of idea. It has been praised for its coherent analysis of 'the undisciplined heart', the phrase in which Annie Strong sums up her youthful, irrational, and amoral feeling, and which stirs David to self-recognition and diagnosis. Almost every character, problem, and episode can be seen as an illustration of this theme. I do not want in any way to deny the novel this unity of subject. It is there, and most explicitly so. What I do want to deny is that the idea, and its unifying function, is a source of strength. G. K. Chesterton, whose criticism combines effusiveness with much insight, said that Dickens's characters were often implausible, but still possessed the power to shake us profoundly. I believe that it is not so much the moral and psychological study of the heart and its training, which gives *David Copperfield* its strength and its vitality, as the intense and local shafts which strike deep as human insights, honest revelations, and dramatic communications.

As a novel of education, I would not put *David Copperfield* in the same class as *Middlemarch*, *The Portrait of a Lady*, or *Sons and Lovers*. These novels show the difficulty of being human, the complexity of human identity and relationship. From reading them, we do not return to a world whose flux and uncertainty

129

is shatteringly different. In *David Copperfield* we are shown a very neat graph of progress: once David sees that his heart is undisciplined, the path ahead is fairly smooth and straight, and Dickens, here as elsewhere, illustrates what seems to me to be a moral and psychological fallacy, the fallacy of identifying diagnosis with remedy. Once Scrooge, Martin Chuzzlewit, David, and Pip arrive at self-knowledge, they can march on to improvement and conversion. Seen as a *Bildungsroman*, the novel's fable shows us very little that carries over into the encounters with life. And the simplifications often rest on evasion within the novel. The actual concept of the disciplined heart seems rather crude, and owes much, I believe, to the impression made on us by another and easier kind of discipline, the discipline of action. We see David's grit and professional industry emerging from the ordeal set him by Betsy Trotwood, his fairy godmother; and by a kind of sideways shift, we may well ignore the absence of much dramatic evidence for the emotional discipline that Annie Strong speaks of. I say 'dramatic evidence': both Annie and David tell of, but do not show, their change of heart. Annie's narrative is a summary of action and feeling, made in retrospect when she confesses to her husband. David's narrative is made to the reader. We are meant to feel and approve David's attempts to discipline his own demands for comfort, rational companionship, and a profound love, and to accept the deficiencies of Dora and of his marriage. Behind the pages of narrative obviously lie the novelist's own hard and fatigued attempts to live with his own marriage. But the toughness and wryness of this experience of accepting uncomfortable life remain unrealized, in terms of the art of fiction. It is dealt with in summary, not shown in action, and though a novelist like Henry James can give to such summary, in the harsh vision of Isabel Archer in *The Portrait of a Lady*, what he himself called 'vivacity', inner action is not Dickens's strength. The report is not only severed from incident, but also undramatic as report. We *see* how he takes his 'woodman's axe' and 'cuts down the trees' until he comes to Dora—here the duplicity of the term 'discipline' is plain, I think—but in the key passages in chapter lviii, 'Domestic', we are only *told* that David gave up the attempts to change his wife. He says that the old unhappy feeling haunted him but was undefined, haunted dreams but did not wreck the present:

> It remained for me to adapt myself to Dora, to share with her what I could, and be happy, to bear on my own shoulders what I must, and be still happy. This was the discipline to which I tried to bring my heart, when I began to think.

Dickens is really only approaching, and then retreating from the idea of showing the disenchanted life. Dora goes on holding his pen, they correspond with Agnes, speculations about another possible life remain outside, conveniently undisturbing. He is touching on a marvellous subject for the psychological novel, but only touching on it.

He chose to summarize, to evade, and then to cut the knot with Dora's death. Many a marital problem in Victorian fiction has to be solved by the Providential death. Dorothea Brooke benefits from this convention every bit as much as David Copperfield: it was left for

Henry James, in *The Portrait of a Lady*, to refuse to cut the knot as Dickens and George Eliot had done, but before we praise him too highly at their expense, we should remember that he finished the novel before showing us Isabel Archer's undismissed marriage.

Both George Eliot and Charles Dickens knew in their own experience the pains of enduring an unloving marriage, she through Lewes's marriage, Dickens through his own. In recognizing the author's invocation of his own Providential plot-control to kill off Dora and lead the way to Agnes, we cannot simply refer to conventions in fiction. Convention and personal fantasy meet here: we are accustomed to speak of the maturity of great art, to see works of art as therapeutic, to applaud the use of technique as discovery, to equate good art with objectified feeling, and bad art with the gratifications of fantasy. Such standards leave us with a handful of novelists and even with these we will find spots of commonness, even with them it may often be the sparsity of biographical materials which makes us speak confidently about their powers of objective realization. All I should like to say here is that some artists, like Charlotte Brontë, and Dickens, work very close to life in some respects, and very far away from it in others. The so-called autobiographical novel is likely to contain chunks of actual report (the school in *Jane Eyre*, the reading, childhood isolation, and neglect in *David Copperfield*) and episodes of wish-fulfilling fantasy (the union with Rochester in *Jane Eyre* and the death of Dora and the marriage with Agnes). We might add the childhood parts of *The Mill on the Floss* and the final union with Tom. It is significant that these novels tend to employ two distinct modes, one a realistic, the other a fantastic, often vaguely religious and idealized symbolic mode. Here are three novels where, we are tempted to say, the psychological realism is confined to the childhood sections, the fantasy of symbol and convenient plotting for the adult section. This is only roughly true: there are moments in the adult sections of all three where truth and subtlety are operative. The pressure of fantasy need not always show itself in vagueness or authorial magic of the kind which produces deaths and conversions and happy marriages at the wave of a wand.

In *David Copperfield* fantasy is at work, shaping relationships, feelings, and climaxes that belong to dreams and wishes, and that tend to lie outside the clear scrutiny of the shaping artist and the self-critical man. It is particularly difficult to communicate and criticize what our longings create: the 'Eureka-feeling', the sense of romantic affinity, and the relief at the end of struggle, all contribute to the religiosity and unparticularized feeling in this novel. Dickens invokes both religious and natural symbolism to express the desires and their wished fulfilments: it is in the Alps, amongst grandeur, isolation, and elevation, away from 'the world', that he discovers the rock on which his love is founded. The very image of the rock is significantly both Wordsworthian and Biblical. We may well borrow other men's profundities and sublimities to convey what we most want and least know. As Arnold Bennett said, the writer's craft is open to many temptations. Dickens is not the only artist to use his art to reflect and distort and re-create an unsatisfied life.

DAVID COPPERFIELD

The results are not only inflated and unconvincing symbols and actions. What are we to say of the comic transformation of the feckless and ponderous Mr Dickens, Senior, into Micawber, and the comic conflation of Dickens's wife and his sweetheart, Maria Beadnell, in the figure of Dora. Dickens uses comedy in the reforming of experience by fantasy. We should note that it is reformed: he was conscious enough of the biographical elements in the novel, and as with most artists, there were some of these elements which he most skilfully controlled and disguised. The real Mrs Dickens wrote a cookery book when she was sixteen and, as Margaret Lane observes in an essay in her book, *Purely for Pleasure* (London, 1966), 'would have had no patience with Dora Copperfield'. While we talk crudely of the gratifications of killing off a wife in fiction, we must also recognize the disguises which imagination can put on, consciously or unconsciously.

We may say that Dickens was dealing with a theme, or adopting a pattern, to which his genius was not suited, or we may say that the closeness of the novel to his discontents and desires made the large moral pattern one very difficult for him to substantiate. However, as I said earlier, this does not mean that the novel has no psychological interest. The psychological interest tends to be rather erratic, appearing in spots rather than stretches, especially once we follow David into the adult world, but it is arrestingly present. I would pick out small details first. In the chapter I have mentioned, 'Domestic', where there is so much summary and evasion, we find revealing and moving dialogue with Dora, which shows how good Dickens can be when he is reticent. David tells her in terms that are perhaps as tactful as the subject allows, that he has been trying to change her, has seen his error, and has decided not 'to try any more'. Dora's response is one of the many small details that make her character more subtle than most critical accounts of it admit:

'It's better for me to be stupid than uncomfortable, isn't it?' said Dora.
'Better to be naturally Dora than anything else in the world.'
'In the world! Ah Doady, it's a large place!'

One moment like this is more delicate and moving than all the loudly whispered hints about her last talk with Agnes. The reader who responds to the novel should be alert to this side of its treatment of people—the reticence, the suggestion, the feather-movement. Other fine moments are of course less quiet. Take, for instance, the night when Uriah Heep sleeps in David's room, a scene dramatically conveying the physical revulsion inseparable from the jealousy which helps to give the adult David the sexual dimension he mostly lacks. In a sense, this episode reminds one of Conrad's *The Secret Sharer*, and taken in combination with the parallels in David's position and Uriah's—poor boys struggling upwards—and with the sexual gloating of Uriah and the lofty purity of David's attitude to Agnes, seems to suggest a kind of Id/Super-Ego tension. I would not suggest that we take this very far, but the relationship between the two men seems to reveal more than is ever made explicit, and the study of David's loathing for Uriah is one of the most powerful insights in the novel. (I do not know if anyone has observed the Biblical origins of their names, but I would suppose that this was an instance where Dickens was not conscious of all the ironies of the associations: Agnes is as far from Bathsheba as Molly Bloom from Penelope, but David certainly wins her from Uriah.) Dickens's treatment of David's feeling for Uriah and Steerforth is much more moving, I suppose because more particularized, than his treatment of the feeling for Dora and Agnes, in the one case distanced by comedy, in the other inflated by a compound of ideals.

I make this brief mention of such moving psychological detail for two reasons: first, because I have criticized the subtlety and interest of the central psychological theme of the undisciplined heart, and must make it plain that I do not consider that Dickens is incapable of treating emotion and relationship; second, because I may be in danger of suggesting that the novel's comic mode is its only source of strength. In fact, the comedy is involved in the weaknesses, too, if only in a negative sense. Those characters in Dickens who are totally exempt from comedy tend to be the unrealized and insubstantial creatures: David himself, like Micawber, Traddles, and Betsy Trotwood, has a vitality that seems in part to derive from the exposure to comic, as well as to serious, analysis. But the comic parts of the novel make a strong contribution to local effect: the vitality of farce and language is both brilliantly funny in details of scene and character, and excellently imitative. Dickens's jokes do not explode and leave no trace. When Micawber speaks, the style is the man:

'Under the impression,' said Mr Micawber, 'that your peregrinations in this metropolis have not as yet been extensive, and that you might have some difficulty in penetrating the arcana of the Modern Babylon in the direction of the City Road—in short,' said Mr Micawber, in another burst of confidence, 'that you might lose yourself—I shall be happy to call this evening, and instal you in the knowledge of the nearest way.'

Micawber's celebrated 'in short' does not merely show up the inflation and grandiose circumlocution of his great flights, it cuts them short, and modifies their grandiosity. The really hollow men in Dickens, like Chadband in *Bleak House*, irritate the reader into deflating and translating their flights; Micawber's very lack of hollowness is shown in his ability to deflate himself, and the stylistic deflation that follows the 'in short' almost always signals the descent to practical matters. The reader who properly attends to the style will not feel too startled at Micawber's final triumphs. The comedy here, as in other characters, is subtly deceptive and subtly revealing. The reader has to learn, with David, to see beneath the comic simplifications, to learn, for instance, that Mrs Micawber's elasticity is not simply comic, but guarantees her much-vaunted but far from hollow constancy, or that Betsy Trotwood's comic spinsterishness has more in it than meets the eye. Dickens is learning to use comedy, not simply for farce and satire, but characteristically, and most originally, to create surface effects and then trip us into feeling the depths beneath. His apparently endstopped jokes, and his apparently static caricatures, are dynamic and complex.

This kind of comedy is appropriately used in a novel of memory, a novel which explores the past, re-enacts it, and explores its meanings. The past sensations and feelings are presented as things remembered, and the effect of the double vision of David the past child, and David the man in the present, works in the same way as the comic duplicity. The rhythm of the novel depends largely on the relation between the time past and time present, a relation which is made very emphatic in the several 'Retrospects' where, by a stroke of what I would call linguistic imagination, Dickens uses the present tense to express what is most visibly presented as the rapid passing of time in the past, a present tense which speaks with a sad and faintly mocking voice of what was vivid and now has faded, a perfect vehicle for all the ironies of nostalgic remembering, reliving, questioning, and burying. Some of the most complex writing, which blends comedy and pathos, is in these passages, and it is in them, I believe, that the strongest source of the novel's unity is revealed. *David Copperfield* is a chronicle of 'the silent gliding on of ... existence', the memory of 'the unseen, unfelt progress of ... life', of 'the river', and 'the journey'; and the gliding is halted, the progress held up, the river stopped, and the journey interrupted, in these four great punctuating chapters, arrestingly coming at the ends of instalments, where the theme is stated, the summary made, the symbol movingly created out of that 'historic present' which uses the language of time present to dramatize time past. It is the unity of feeling, that concept of form used by Schlegel and Coleridge to answer the rigidities of their neo-classical predecessors, that seems most appropriately invoked to describe the structure, the subject, and the appeal of *David Copperfield*.

138

7 *Great Expectations*

We all know that food has a special place in the novels of Dickens. He loves feasts and scorns fasts. His celebration of the feast is not that of the glutton or the gourmet: eating and drinking are valued by him as proofs of sociability and gusto, but more important still, as ceremonies of love. The conversion of Scrooge is marked by his present of a goose to Bob Cratchit and his reunion at his nephew's table: both the giving and the participation show his newly found ability to love. The Christmas dinner and the geniality of the English pub are not sentimentalized as isolated institutions of goodwill, conveniently cut off from the poverty and hunger outside the window. Good housekeeping is proved by nourishing and well-ordered meals, and Mrs Jellyby cannot feed her family properly; but the same is true of the bleak housekeeping of England, which cannot feed Jo or the brickmasters. Chadband's superfluous feasts are put beside Jo's hunger and Guster's loving crust to qualify the approval of good appetite. The social emphasis in *Great Expectations* is rather different from that of *Bleak House*, but in both novels, and elsewhere, the same moral values are attached to meals—to the giving, receiving, eating, and serving of food. These values might be summed up as good appetite without greed, hospitality without show, and ceremony without pride or condescension. Pip's deterioration and change of heart are shown in terms of these values.

All these values are shown, positively and negatively, in the meals in *Great Expectations*. Food is used to define various aspects of love, pride, social ambition, and gratitude, and the meals are often carefully placed in order to underline and explain motivation and development. Dickens's attitude to food has no doubt considerable biographical interest. Dickens—deprived child, food-lover, great talker, oral type—juxtaposes Mrs Joe's pincushion breast and her dispensation of bread, and this may well be his grimmest attack on the maternal image. But in spite of this grotesque instance, I believe that the generalized association of food and love in Dickens strikes us less by its neurotic fantasy than by its use of what we all feel to be the natural appropriateness of the metaphor 'hunger' when it is used of love. I do not call the meals in *Great Expectations* symbols: their affirmation of value seems to involve no conceptual transference and little heightening. It is our awareness of the Last Supper which often tempts us to describe this kind of significant meal as symbolic (the meal shared by Bartle Massey and Adam Bede in the upper room is a good example) but the Last Supper (like the Passover and other ritual feasts) became an effective symbol, in part at least, because it tapped the significance of ordinary communion—the eating, giving, and receiving, in public, amongst friends and associates. The meals in Dickens convey no more, I suggest, than the elementary implications of natural domestic and social order, given particularity by the context of the novel. The generalizations which the meals in *Great Expectations* carry involve none of the transference associated with symbolism, nothing of the movement from a first term to a second which is involved in our reading of the symbol of the wild waves, the fog, or the prison. There is certainly an accumulation of significance in *Great Expectations*, and we may come to expect that when characters sit down to eat there will be more than a furtherance of action, local colour, or comic play. We come to expect some extension or qualification of the moral significance already correlated with the meals. This is an extension of the particular definition of character, a way of emphasizing the connections and distances between different characters or different events, showing the irony and necessity of the internal moral pattern. The meals themselves are charged with no more than the moral significances of everyday life, where good mothers feed their children lovingly but not excessively or demandingly; where meals are sociable occasions; where good manners are desirable but not all that important; where theft may be condoned if the thief is starving; where there is something distasteful about the host or mother or cook whose meals are merely boasts; where there is something meretricious in the splendid feast which is strikingly different from the routine meals of the same household; where abstinence may be either unhealthy or unselfish.

The first meal in *Great Expectations* is *demanded* in the first chapter. Magwitch in desperate hunger terrifies Pip into stealing food: 'You know what wittles is ... you get me wittles.' In the third chapter Pip brings the food, and Magwitch makes the first response of

141

gratitude which begins the long chain of obligation, illusion, pride, and love. It is necessary to see what moves his gratitude: it is not the mere provision of food, important though this is. Pip is doing more than satisfy the physical need, he is allowing nature more than nature needs. Magwitch is eating like a beast but Pip treats him as a guest and makes him respond as a guest:

He was already handing mincemeat down his throat in the most curious manner—more like a man who was putting it away somewhere in a violent hurry, than a man who was eating it—but he left off to take some of the liquor. He shivered all the while so violently, that it was quite as much as he could do to keep the neck of the bottle between his teeth, without biting it off...

He was gobbling mincemeat, meat bone, bread, cheese, and pork pie, all at once: staring distrustfully while he did so at the mist all round us, and often stopping—even stopping his jaws—to listen.

This is a grotesque table, spread in the wilderness of mist and marshes for a man who is wolfing down the food out of fear. Pip is no more in the conventional position of host than Magwitch is in the conventional position of guest, but the very lack of ceremony moves Pip to do more than steal and give in terror and in minimal satisfaction of need. Pity moves him to sauce the meat with ceremony and turn it into something more than Lady Macbeth's 'bare meeting'. Just as Lady Macbeth's rebuke has special point because it is made at a great feast to the host who is a guest-murderer, so Pip's ceremony has special point in this bare rough meeting where the guest is desperate and the host terrorized:

Pitying his desolation ... I made bold to say, 'I am glad you enjoy it'.

'Did you speak?'

'I said, I am glad you enjoyed it.'

'Thankee, my boy. I do.'

The child's civility and pity take no offence from his guest's table-manners. These are carefully observed, without revulsion:

I had often watched a large dog of ours eating his food; and now I noticed a decided similarity between the dog's way of eating, and the man's. The man took strong sharp sudden bites, just like the dog. He swallowed, or rather snapped up, every mouthful, too soon and too fast; and he looked sideways here and there while he ate, as if he thought there was danger in every direction of somebody's coming to take the pie away. He was altogether too unsettled in his mind over it, to appreciate it comfortably, I thought, or to have anybody to dine with him, without making a chop with his jaws at the visitor. In all of which particulars he was very like the dog.

The detached account makes the politeness more marked. It is apparent that Pip's naïve comparisons, to the dog and to more comfortable meals, imply no sense of social superiority, though the social implications are plain to the reader. Pip is not repelled by the resemblance to the dog, but is sorry for it, and instead of treating the man like a dog, gives with love. The 'I am glad you enjoy it' and the 'Thankee' turn the rudest meal in the novel into an introductory model of ceremony. What makes the ceremony is love, generosity, and gratitude. I need not labour the attachment of this scene to the main themes of the novel.

This meal acts as a model of ceremony, and controls

our response to the many related descriptions of meals which succeed it. The gratitude and compassionate love are both present in chapter v, when Magwitch lies about stealing the food, to protect Pip, and is answered by Joe: 'God knows you're welcome to it—so far as it was ever mine. ... We don't know what you have done, but we wouldn't have you starved to death for it, poor miserable fellow-creatur.—Would us, Pip?'

This in its turn evokes another response of gratitude —an inarticulate working of the throat—from Magwitch. The first small links are forged in Pip's chain 'of iron or gold, of thorns or flowers'.

It is not until much later, in chapter xxxviii, that Pip sees that this is where his chain really begins, 'before I knew that the world held Estella'. The actual image is narrowed down, in the next chapter, to the 'wretched gold and silver chains' with which Magwitch has loaded him. When the image of the chain first appears (in the singular) it has no connection with the convict for Pip sees its beginning in his encounter with Miss Havisham and Estella, in Satis House. The beginning of his illusory great expectations, like the beginning of the real ones, is marked by a significant meal. Estella is the hostess, Pip the guest. The meal is less grotesque than the meal with Magwitch but it too lacks the ceremonious cover of a roof, for Estella tells Pip to wait in the yard:

She came back, with some bread and meat and a little mug of beer. She put the mug down on the stones of the yard, and gave me the bread and meat without looking at me, as insolently as if I were a dog in disgrace. I was so humiliated, hurt, spurned, offended, angry, sorry—I cannot hit upon the right name for the smart—God knows what its name was—that tears started to my eyes. (ch. viii)

The contrast is clinched by the comparison with the dog. Pip's full wants are not satisfied, even though this is the hospitality of Satis House, but in terms of physical need he is given enough. He is treated like a dog, given no more than nature needs, but he does not lose his appetite, any more than Magwitch, treated with courtesy, stops eating like a dog. Dickens makes this distinction unsentimentally and truthfully, merely allowing Pip to observe that 'the bread and food were acceptable, and the beer was warming and tingling, and I was soon in spirits to look about me'. Like Magwitch, and for similar reasons of protective love, Pip lies about this meal. His sense of humiliation and his desire to protect Estella from 'the contemplation of Mrs Joe' makes him elaborate the marvellous childish fantasy about the 'cake and wine on gold plates', which Pumble-chook and Joe and Mrs Joe, in their social innocence, accept. Pip invents a meal appropriate to Satis House, and hides his shame, but he preserves both the hier-archy and the bizarre quality of his encounter by placing the meal in a coach, and saying that he 'got up behind the coach to eat mine, because she told me to'. Even the dog comes back, magnified into 'four im-mense dogs' who come off rather better than Pip did since they fight 'for veal-cutlets out of a silver basket'. On his next visit to Satis House we return briefly to the dog: 'I was taken into the yard to be fed in the former dog-like manner.' The two meals respond in perfect antithesis.

The first ceremony of love finds another responsive

scene when Magwitch discloses his responsibility and motivation to Pip. We are carefully reminded of the first meal on the marshes: 'I drops my knife many a time in that hut when I was a eating my dinner or my supper, and I says, "Here's the boy again, a looking at me whiles I eats and drinks!" ' (ch. xxxix).

It is to this actual memory of the meal that he attaches his plan to 'make that boy a gentleman' but when the gentleman serves him with a meal he does not look at him as the boy did:

> He ate in a ravenous manner that was very disagreeable, and all his actions were uncouth, noisy, and greedy. Some of his teeth had failed him since I saw him eat on the marshes, and as he turned his food in his mouth, and turned his head sideways to bring his strongest fangs to bear upon it, he looked terribly like a hungry old dog.
> If I had begun with any appetite, he would have taken it away, and I should have sat much as I did—repelled from him by an insurmountable aversion, and gloomily looking at the cloth. (ch. xl)

The uncouth eating, the hunger, the sideways movement, and the comparison with the dog are repetitions from the early scene which emphasize the distance between the child and the man. This time the observation is full of revulsion, the food is not sauced with ceremony. But if the host has changed, the guest has not, and he apologizes for his doglike eating with undoglike courtesy:

> 'I'm a heavy grubber, dear boy,' he said, as a polite kind of apology when he had made an end of his meal, 'but I always was. If it had been in my constitution to be a lighter grubber, I might ha' got into lighter trouble.'

The apology is made without shame or self-pity on the part of Magwitch, and provokes no sympathy on the part of Pip. In the early scene the child's pity was impulsive and provoked simply by the desperate eating and panic. In the later scenes, Pip is in a position to see the connection between the heavy grubbing and the heavy trouble, but describes without pity the roughness and greed: 'there was Prisoner, Felon, Bondsman, plain as plain could be'.

The next meal is described without emphasis. We are told that Magwitch wipes his knife on his leg, but by now Pip is too concerned to hear the convict's history to have room for shame and revulsion. The very last meal described—supper on the night before the attempted escape—contains no comment on manners or response: 'It was a dirty place enough ... but there was a good fire in the kitchen, and there were eggs and bacon to eat, and various liquors to drink' (ch. liv).

By now Pip's pride has been entirely subdued to the need for action. The quiet disappearance of comment testifies to the naturalness and literalness of the scenes of eating and drinking: a series of related scenes has been established, bringing out the moral significance of needs and hospitality and good manners, but it is brought to no formal climax. There is no explicit comment on the irrelevance of good manners in the crisis of need, no reminiscence of the fellowship of the first meal and the first occasion when Pip helped Magwitch to escape his pursuers, nothing of the climactic recognition of symbolism which we find in James's dove, or Lawrence's rainbow, or Dickens's own wild waves. The meals are only tapped for their moral significance on occasions when men need food desperately or when there is scope for hospitality: towards the end of the story the meals are inartifically subordinated to other features of the action. I do not make this distinction in order to decry the more contrived symbolism in other novels, but merely in order to bring out Dickens's unheightened and sober reliance on everyday moral and social facts. There is, I think, no question of an unconscious moral pattern, for the repetition of details makes the control quite plain, but Dickens is content to subdue this significant series of meals to the proportions and emphases of his story.

With the same almost unobtrusive reflection of ordinary moral fact, the meals with Estella are also described without schematic arrangement. They scarcely develop into a pattern, and Dickens can allow himself to describe a meal without relating it to earlier significances. When Estella and Pip have tea together in the hotel, or when Pip does eventually dine with some ceremony inside Satis House, no moral emphasis is present: on the first occasion Dickens is concerned to develop aspects of the relationship to which need and ceremony are irrelevant; on the second he is concerned with the tense understatement of Jaggers's observation of Estella. But although some of the meals in this novel make no moral definition, it is true that nearly all the characters and families are given, at some point, their significant ceremony of food. Magwitch tells Pip and Herbert how his heavy grubbing explains his troubled career and begins his life-story with the little boy who stole turnips and who was always driven by the need 'to put something into his stomach'. Pip as a child is not physically deprived in this way, but although he is given enough to eat, he is not given his food with love. In Chapter ii, between Magwitch's demand for food and Pip's generous response, we are given a glimpse of Mrs Joe's 'bringing up by hand'. She is an unloving mother-surrogate who feeds her family unceremoniously:

My sister had a trenchant way of cutting our bread-and-butter for us, that never varied. First, with her left hand she jammed the loaf hard and fast against her bib—where it sometimes got a pin into it, and sometimes a needle, which we afterwards got into our mouths. Then she took some butter (not too much) on a knife and spread it on the loaf, in an apothecary kind of way, as if she were making a plaister—using both sides of the knife with a slapping dexterity, and trimming and moulding the butter off round the crust. Then, she gave the knife a final smart wipe on the edge of the plaister ...

The pins and needles have already been mentioned as characteristic of this unmotherly breast: 'She was tall and bony, and almost always wore a coarse apron, fastened over her figure behind with two loops, and having a square impregnable bib in front, that was stuck full of pins and needles.'

Some of the implications of this juxtaposition are terrifying, but the Gargery household is treated with comedy rather than with the harsh violence which is the medium for the Murdstones. But both the comic mode and the grim seem at times to draw freely on Dickens's fantasy. The moral implications within the novel are plain: Mrs Joe gives unlovingly, to put it mildly, taking most pleasure in the administration of Tar-Water and fasts, while Joe shares the wedges of bread in love and play, and tries to make up for Pip's sufferings at the Christmas dinner with spoonfulls of gravy.

The cold comfort of Mrs Joe's meals, like her uncomfortable cleanliness, makes her an ancestress of Mrs Ogmore-Pritchard, though Dickens inflicts a terrible revenge on her in the action. She has the front-parlour mentality, and the only ceremony in the Gargery household, apart from the rough meals shared by Pip and Joe, is the false ceremony of hospitality. Her showing-off at the dinner-party contrasts rudely with her earlier words to Joe and Pip: 'I ain't a going to have no formal cramming and busting and washing-up now', and they have their slices served out as if they 'were two thousand troops on a forced march instead of a man and boy at home'. I need not dwell on the Christmas dinner, with Mr Wopsle's theatrical declamation of grace, with the adjurations to Pip to be grateful 'to them which brought you up by hand', with Pumble-chook's immodest generosity and gluttony and the comic nemesis when he chokes on the Tar-Water. The contrast between the ceremony of love and the false ceremony is there, together with the rebuke of starvation. For Magwitch has eaten the pie and drunk the brandy. This is underlined when Pip observes Pumble-chook's possessive appropriation of the wine he has given to Mrs Joe and his generous treating of the flattering sergeant. The false giving and receiving are put in the context of the first meal with Magwitch when Pip comments, 'I thought what terrible good sauce for a dinner my fugitive friend on the marshes was.'

Pip's humiliation by Estella is also put into a larger context when he explains that his susceptibility to injustice and shame was attributable to the unloving home. Joe makes even the hacked bread and superfluous gravy the food of love, but Estella sharpens the sense of false ceremony, in part by denying ceremony, and Pip becomes less conscious of love's seasoning than of good manners. He continues in fantasy, and eventually moves from the back of the coach. The actual social significance of eating habits becomes emphatic in a novel about snobbery and aspiration, and there are other meals which raise the question of love and ceremony. When Pip has his first meal with Herbert Pocket, a difficult social situation is eased by Herbert's friendly delicacy, and he gives both the strawberries and the lessons in etiquette with true ceremony. This is a scene which establishes both the importance of good manners and the importance of love. It contrasts strongly with the second meal with Magwitch, where Pip is the bad host, and is paralleled by the first, when Pip is the true host. It is closest of all to another scene, where Herbert and Pip are entertaining Joe to breakfast. Joe is 'stiff from head to foot', cannot say outright that he prefers tea to coffee, and is as self-conscious in his politeness as Magwitch is unself-conscious in his roughness:

Then he fell into such unaccountable fits of meditation, with his fork midway between his plate and his mouth; had his eyes attracted in such strange directions; was afflicted with such remarkable coughs; sat so far from the table, and dropped so much more than he ate, and pretended he hadn't dropped it; that I was heartily glad when Herbert left us for the city. (ch. xxvii)

This failure in hospitality—'I had neither the good

sense nor the good feeling to know that this was all my fault'—prepares us for the greater failure, the greater social gulf, and the greater shame, when Magwitch returns and Pip makes a first false, but healthy, comparison between his shame for Joe and his shame before the convict, for whom he had deserted Joe.

There are other scenes, more or less emphatic, in which the social values of eating are defined. There is the false show, lightly touched on, in the last celebratory supper at the forge before Pip leaves home, when he sits ashamed in his splendour for their delight and they are all 'very low' despite roast fowl and flip. This contrasts with another kind of false show, in the same chapter, when Mr Pumblechook flatters and celebrates in a travesty of the love-feast. He toasts Pip in extravagant mock-abasement when he toasts Pip—'May I?— *may* I?'—and elaborately deprecates the chicken and tongue—'one or two little things had round from the Boar, that I hope you may not despise'—and apostrophizes the fowl—'Ah! poultry, poultry! You little thought ... when you was a young fledgling, what was in store for you' (ch. xix). At the other social extreme from this exhibition of hospitable abasement, but close to it morally, is Pip's little fantasy, at the beginning of the same chapter, of feasting the villagers, 'bestowing a dinner of roast-beef and plum-pudding, a pint of ale, and a gallon of condescension'. There are many other details which might be mentioned: the funeral repast after Mrs Joe's death, Jaggers's good food and ruthless hospitality, the geniality of the pub, Pip's susceptibility to wine on one or two occasions, the lavishness of his housekeeping with Herbert, and the ordered, warm, and unpretentious hospitality of Wemmick.

Almost all characters and groups are given moral and social definition by their attitudes to food and hospitality. Old Barley keeps the provisions in his room, and provides Clara with bread and cheese while he has mutton-chops, potatoes, and split pease stewed up in butter; he roars and bangs for his grog and growls in pain while trying to cut through a Double Gloucester with his gouty hand. The ill-fed children are the unloved children. The baby Pocket, like Pip, is endangered by being fed on pins, though in his case the inappropriate food is the result of neglect and disorder not of an aggressive display of good housekeeping. The disorder, bad economy, and inadequate meals of the Pocket family are another version of the neglected Jellybys in *Bleak House*, and just as Mrs Jellyby is ironically exposed as a model of displaced charity, so Mrs Pocket is shown in her disorder as another qualification of class-distinction and great expectations. Her delusions of grandeur lead to the disregard of proper ceremony. Although each bad mother is attached to the special theme of each novel, the basic moral failure is the same. It is a failure in love.

I have not yet mentioned one of the most prominent failures in love in *Great Expectations*. This is Miss Havisham's failure. Her love-feast is preserved in its decay to make the most conspicuous contribution to the themes of love and nature. Nothing remains of the expectations of Satis House but a gruesome parody of ceremony:

The most prominent object was a long table with a tablecloth spread on it, as if a feast had been in preparation when the house and the clocks all stopped together. An *épergne* or centre-piece of some kind was in the middle of this cloth; it was so heavily overhung with cobwebs that its form was quite undistinguishable; and as I looked along the yellow expanse out of which I remember its seeming to grow, like a black fungus, I saw speckled-legged spiders with blotchy bodies running home to it ... (ch. xi)

Miss Havisham makes a symbolic correlation between the mouldering wedding-breakfast and her own life. She has been gnawed by pain as the food has been gnawed by mice, she has worn away with the meal, and when she is dead she too will be laid out on that table, where she has allocated the places for her predatory family to sit and 'feast upon' her. The betrayal of love and the hypocritical greedy show of love are both bracketed as false ceremony in this grisly image of transubstantiation. The ghastly conceit stands out from Dickens's other significant correlations of love and food as a product of a diseased fancy and an impossible attempt to pervert nature. Jaggers makes explicit the other implications of the stasis and decay which relate this meal to the pattern of normal routine and relationship:

He asked me how often I had seen Miss Havisham eat and drink ...
I considered, and said, 'Never'. 'And never will, Pip,' he retorted, with a frowning smile. 'She has never allowed herself to be seen doing either, since she lived this present life of hers. She wanders about in the night, and then lays hands on such food as she takes.' (ch. xxix)

Miss Havisham's rejection of ordinary public meals is like her attempt to shut out the daylight. Food in

Great Expectations, as in *Macbeth*, is part of the public order, and the meals testify to human need and dependence, and distinguish false ceremony from the ceremony of love. They are not literary symbols but natural demonstrations. Pip's change of heart is a change from the unconditioned act of love to this contaminated false ceremony and back again to the Dickensian natural man. Like Scrooge, he demonstrates the vulnerable virtue by loss and gain.